HOW TO TENNIS

think, train, and
compete to your potential

HOW TO TENNIS

think, train, and
compete to your potential

Beau Treyz

Copyright 2020 © by Beau Treyz

All rights reserved under the Pan-American and International Copyright Conventions. This book may not be reproduced in whole or in part, in any form or by any means electronic or mechanical, including photocopying, recording, or by any information storage and retrieval system now known or hereinafter invented, without written permission of the author.
Cover Illustration by C.S. Fritz
Book Design by Albatross Design Co.

CONTENTS

ACKNOWLEDGEMENTS —————————————— 1
FOREWORD BY KELLY JONES ————————— 3
INTRODUCTION ————————————————— 5
   ONE: EXPLANATION OF ABCD ——————— 13
   TWO: WINNERS AND UNFORCED ERRORS — 25
   THREE: SKILLING, NOT DRILLING ———— 31
   FOUR: TRAINING THE MINIMUMS ———— 37
   FIVE: INDULGENCES ———————————— 47
   SIX: REALISTIC WAYS TO TRAIN ————— 55
   SEVEN: MENTALITY OF B&C ——————— 67
   EIGHT: TALKIN BOUT PRACTICE ———— 73
   NINE: CONCLUSION ————————————— 85
BIBLIOGRAPHY ————————————————— 89

ACKNOWLEDGEMENTS

To mom and dad for a lifetime of commitment and sacrifices. Teaching me how to be who I want to be, and the efforts that would take. For always answering my calls, for encouraging me and being there for me through good times, bad times and Valentimes.

To Kelly Jones and Chuck Brymer, for embracing me and my ideas while I was a young coach. You both taught me so much about the game, and the industry that is tennis coaching; thank you for continuing to be men I can rely on.

To all the players I've coached, thank you for trusting me. For going with me down rabbit holes, and trusting that I always have your best interest in mind. Coaching you guys has been a fulfillment of my dreams, and I'm happy to have helped you on your way towards achieving your own dreams.

To tennis, for giving me something to go after. Tennis has taken me across the world and introduced me to lifelong friends as well as taught me lifelong lessons.

FOREWORD
BY KELLY JONES

It was in the fall of 2019 when I met Beau Treyz for the first time. He was traveling and coaching Brandon Nakashima, one of the emerging young American tennis players touted to be the next Grand Slam Champion. Beau and I were assigned together as a team to help Brandon develop the tools to get through the very tough road ahead. My role was that of "experienced" coach mentoring the much younger coach who just recently started his tennis coaching career.

My tennis career and journey spans several decades which includes playing 48 Grand Slam events during which time I achieved the #1 ATP Doubles ranking and won 2 ATP Singles Titles. I have been fortunate to have coached James Blake, Mardy Fish, John Isner and other ATP, WTA players. During this time I also developed very young boys and girls that reached top 100 in the world. The reason for sharing this is to help the reader decide if my review of Beau's book is credible

I am a pretty tough critic when it comes to coaches opinions about how to play the game technically or tactically. I love to learn but am not impressed unless I hear something that makes sense or something I haven't heard before. I have spent a lot of time with some of the greatest tennis minds in the game and have blended many of these great ideas with my own theories. I never imagined that my partnership with Beau would wake me up to a whole new world of how to help players play their best tennis.

After our initial on court session it became clear that Beau as an unassuming, respectful and great person was not your average young coach trying to make a name for himself. He was professional and mature beyond his age and I have said before that I do not know anyone more professional or knowledgeable than Beau. His dedication to learning how to play your best self (beat your equal) is unmatched in my opinion. Our personalities and moral compass were very similar and I enjoyed sharing my knowledge with him as the "experienced" one in the hopes of helping him become a great coach.

Upon our first few weeks together I was so impressed with Beau's professionalism, ethical compass and desire to be a great coach. I had no idea how much time and research he had already put forth in establishing his coaching philosophy and tactical analysis of how players need to think and train to play their best tennis at all levels. He has developed a tactical formula in his book on "how to beat your equal". His advice will change the way coach's coach, review video and how you scout your opponents. In the end, I'm sure I learned more from him than he did from me.

INTRODUCTION

My goal as a coach, and for this book, is to help players grow their skills, understand how to use them in matches, and build toward their potential. I've spent most of my life playing and coaching tennis; I'm well-acquainted with practice days with dad, bus rides with my teammates, big wins, and brutal losses. I've lived a sports life, and now I want to share some of what I've learned.

A match I lost at a Futures Tournament in Stellenbosch, South Africa, stands out in my mind as the starting point for this book. It was a tight match. My opponent had a better ranking than I did; we both played great, but I didn't win. After the match, I felt like I needed to have more in my game. I knew it wasn't all physical ability that helped him win, but I didn't yet understand what the mental and emotional parts were. I didn't know how to structure my practices or what areas of my game to focus on the most. I was putting in the time, making the sacrifices, but I didn't have the information I needed.

This match was back in 2015 when I played Futures coachless and on my own dime, right after graduating from the University of Nebraska. College tennis had taught me invaluable lessons, given me lifelong friendships, and was one hundred percent the right decision for me given my playing ability. But it did not prepare me to be a professional: I rarely had individualized coaching, and if I did, it was more about how to win matches at my spot in the lineup than it was about developing my game for the pro circuit. So I was more or less clueless when I started playing Futures. I would work hard on court, diet, and fitness, but I wasn't ready to improve mentally the way I needed to. **I looked at the other players and wondered how some guys were winning so consistently, even though the entire tournament was full of players of similar levels. We were all good enough to practice together, but the same few guys always won the matches. This book's ideas came from me figuring out how to beat my equal--my approach to old problems that plague tennis players of all levels.**

    I wanted to feel relaxed, confident, and strategic when I was on court playing matches. Back then, I would panic too quickly, either because I was playing poorly or because I didn't have a good strategy. Mentally, I was rarely relaxed during matches. When you're not settled, it's hard to feel confident. To me, Settled means that I know what my level is, I know what I can expect in the match, and I'm ready to do my best. I can be excited or mad in a moment of the match and still be 'settled' overall. I wanted to be confident in my level of execution, my fitness, and my gameplan. And I wanted to be playing 'pro style' tennis. I think most players feel this same way.

    My mindset was something like, 'I want to play the type of tennis that will get me to the Top 100.' In tennis, that often conjures a different picture for every player. To me, there was a difference between playing to win these Futures matches and playing to develop my game to hold up against the best competition on the planet. I remember feeling like I needed a whole new foundation in my game: how I strategized, how I thought, and how I could put my best game on the court when it mattered. My understanding of what I needed to do to become relaxed, confident, and strategic was off, and I knew it deep down. This book is for players that feel the same way.

    Some of the most important matches in a tennis player's career happen against your equal- where your serve is no longer a massive weapon, and your forehand doesn't do as much damage as you're accustomed to. These matches require you to do something different. **They demand your full physical, mental and emotional engagement, which is what we should be training for.** It's rewarding to play your equals because they challenge you mentally, physically, and emotionally. There's more to the match when your opponent can challenge you than when the outcome is a foregone conclusion. In high school and college, I became more interested in challenging myself by facing my equal than I was in winning or losing. Pushing myself always made me better by the end of the session, winning and losing didn't. **All I wanted was to improve**.

Once I started thinking about why I liked to play my equal, I understood that it was the competition and the mastery part of tennis that I wanted, not so much the rankings part, which simply describes the result of the competition at a given time. Of course, through playing Futures, I eventually learned that I didn't have what it took to make a proper professional career out of playing tennis, but it wasn't the losing that brought me to this conclusion. Futures show you where you stand if you don't already know. I saw that there were bigger, faster, stronger, better-funded players who had more wisdom being put into their careers than I did. To be able to honestly commit myself to beating players on the ATP Tour, which is where the money is, who are also significantly better than players on the Futures Tour, I knew I had to improve tenfold. There was a point when I realized I didn't have what it took to be a Top 100 player, and I began to shift my focus from 'What can I do to be top 100' to 'What does a Futures guy need to make it to the top 100?'

At Futures, I saw and studied what the top players in the tournaments were doing and how their coaches

were helping them. I also saw the guys who rarely won matches. Every day was like a side-by-side comparison of what to do and what not to do. What I saw was hard workers, but not necessarily smart workers.

Everyone at this level is willing to give their all physically, but rarely was anyone talking about the mental side of tennis or the strategy side. I kept seeing the same drills and the same work ethic, but I never saw those guys breakthrough to the next level, let alone make it to the Top 100. I knew they could be spending their time more productively, and I knew I could help, and so training players to reach their potential became my new goal. I wanted Futures guys to get their shot at ATP's. I always envied the better players because I felt they had a legitimate chance to master their games and make it to the ATP level, which led me to start thinking along the lines of, 'I'd rather master something than be ok at something' and that's when I started thinking about coaching.

One aspect of tennis that has gotten more pronounced to me as I've gone up through the different levels (Juniors, Division 1, Futures, Challengers, ATP events) is how one-off results are exciting, but they rarely make careers. Your skill on the court has to be repeatable. You can't make a career against your equals without mastery. A couple of good wins, or even good weeks, won't get you the consistently top-level results you want and need. The best tennis players in the world are absolute masters. These players are not only masters of every shot they might have to hit, but masters of the way they think and the strategies they use. Maybe 'the most important thing that upper-level tennis players need to focus on is strategy and decision-making.' **To me, it's an understanding of strategy, and decision-making that players need to practice so that they can do it match after match. I hope I can help players master their level and continue getting better through the ideas in this book.**

I wrote this book to help you reach your potential, and to give you the tools to face, and beat, your equals - and even your superiors. Those are the moments that matter; how do you do when things are neither for you nor against you, but are. To me, this is where careers are made, and the true value of sport lies. When you're playing well, you can do anything; and when you're playing poorly, anything can happen. We've all been there, and we've all handled both. But there is an excellent opportunity to be had in these middle moments when things become 'routine'- and in these times you can make a massive jump in your game - 'what do you do when things are 'normal?' For me, that's the critical question that decides a player's trajectory. There will still be momentum swings, but the guy with the higher level throughout the match will typically be the winner.

You can get a lot more out of sports if you think about how they relate to life- you can give them meaning and purpose and start to grow more than just the speed of your forehand. If you think about how you deal with situations on and off the court and then think of how you would like to deal with those situations, your goal is to merge those two. It's about becoming that ideal version of yourself or at least always trying to become that version. It's probably more important to try to become that version than it is to be that version. A part of me wants to search out those 'equal' moments and challenges; I want to face as many of those moments as I can because it's getting through those moments that inspires me and gets me closer to the version of myself that I want to be.

I hope these ideas reach past the tennis court and help you in your life. This is only my first book, with more to come. And I'm sure I will prove and disprove some of the ideas I talk about here because I'm continually refining these ideas. What else is there for me to do besides test these different ideas about how to best push myself and become the best version of me? It doesn't matter if it's tennis, relationships, or boxing, shouldn't we all be trying to become our best selves? It's all about honesty. Only we know our limits and how much we can push ourselves, so whether people tell you you're great, or if they discourage you on your path, it doesn't matter. Only you know what's inside you, and only you can bring it out.

Many of my drills and theories ask players and coaches to use their imagination and patience, just as tennis requires. You have to understand what your mental representations of tennis already are, and how to adjust them. We all have mental representations--for example, imagine the Eiffel Tower. Some of us have been there, others have lived across the street, and others have only seen it in movies; no matter what level of detail you know about the Eiffel Tower, if you can imagine it, then you have a mental representation of it. Naturally, those people with a better mental representation will be more reliable as to what the Eiffel Tower is really like, i.e., how tall it is, etc. The person who lived across the street from it for ten years will have a better mental representation than the person who only saw it in a movie. In tennis, the best players have a thorough mental representation of shot combinations and strategies. They know what shot they're trying to hit and why they're trying to hit it at any given moment in a match; they know the scenario they're in and the mental representation they have of it helps them handle the scenario effectively. Because they've played that scenario through in their heads a thousand times

In tennis, we seldom need to stand on the forehand side and hit balls back and forth cross-court with our opponents, so I rarely practice it. **Serious juniors and professional players should develop their games in the areas of the court that pay the most significant dividends.** I believe competitive players of any level could use the drills and strategies in this book to improve their game, but all of the percentages are based on the men's professional game.

I have seen this approach lead to improvement many times over by now, with players of different ages and abilities. First, I practiced these ideas on myself, and although I didn't get the ranking I dreamed of, I got the growth and improvement. An eight-month period I spent with Gage Brymer at his academy in Irvine, California, was one of the only times in my life that I improved consistently. Gage got the benefits of this training and saw his ranking go from ATP #1978 to #455. He and his father Chuck, do an unbelievable job of finding ways to continue improving.

When I started working with Brandon Nakashima, we had a similar experience of continual improvement that translated into winning more matches. When he left the University of Virginia after playing just one semester, we started working together when his ATP Singles ranking was #942; now, seven months later, he is up to a career-high of #218. Winning matches is all on the player—the man in the arena. **What I am personally proud of is that both guys improved. They legitimately got better at tennis and went towards their potential, and that is my goal no matter what level of player I'm working with; I've had similar experiences working with other professionals and juniors as well. That is the rewarding part for me.**

These ideas have been bouncing around in my head for years, from when I would sit on the bench as a kid and watch my dad and brother train after school, and they're still bouncing around my head now. I've gotten to be around some great tennis minds, and spitball ideas about how to improve skills both physical and mental with people from all different sports and career paths. On my podcast, I've been able to talk with NFL Hall of Famers, NBA players, and great musicians and artists, and nearly all of them harp on the importance of mastery and skill and how they went about mastering their craft.

One of the best memories I have in tennis is my time at the Juan Carlos Ferrero Equelite Academy in Villena, Spain, when I was 14. I went there to train for six weeks over the summer, and one day I saw Ferrero and Guillermo Garcia Lopez training with no one around watching. I went over to the court, sat in the grass, and watched them battle. I wrote down everything they did. I drew out the drills they were doing and wrote down what the coaches were saying. I looked at their intensity. I was in heaven. I still have these drills in a notebook I keep with me, and I go back to it time and again. These six weeks in Villena were transformative for me.

In all my experiences--from playing for the University of Nebraska to late-night talks with other players about what we could do to improve, I've explored and refined these ideas. I have been in some amazing situations, and I've done my best to soak up as much as possible. Now I want to contribute and innovate. I hope this book helps you bring out your best.

ONE
EXPLANATION OF ABCD

The number one thing I wanted to figure out as a player was strategy; I needed to be clear about my gameplan in every match so that I could make adjustments as the match went on. I knew I had to perform at a similar level every match, but I struggled to pull it off; I needed a concrete gameplan that I trusted and could base my game around. I needed evidence for why I was winning and losing. I wanted reasons that applied to every match I played, and I wanted to be able to adjust my gameplan mildly depending on my opponent's strengths and weaknesses. Very often, after matches, I wouldn't know what truly happened; I'd only have an idea, and most of the time, that was skewed by whether I won or lost, which is not the best way to go about improving.

Enter ABCD. ABCD are areas of the court and visual guidelines for us while playing that help make our decisions of where to hit each shot simpler. You can see it better in the chart below. Essentially my entire strategy of how to best play tennis at a pro-level is based around understanding ABCD and how to use the different zones.

After studying over 800 matches on the ATP and Challenger Tours and marking down in which zone each shot lands, I've got these percentages to guide me: A=3%, B = 34%, C=57%, and D=6%. These percentages represent precisely what percentage of shots land in each zone. I've taken every shot into account; returns, volleys, overheads, passing shots, drop shots. While watching, I also found different combinations of ways to take risks. These have shaped my theory on how to win matches for the individual players I work with, but understanding ABCD was the most impactful basic strategy for me.

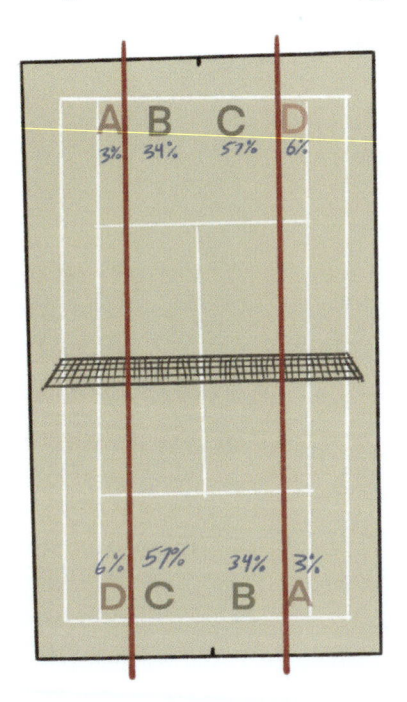

Easy As

What first stood out was that the pros so rarely go to the corners, which is contrary to the belief held by so many players, parents, and coaches. They play 91% of their shots through B&C. And 57% of those shots to their opponent's backhand. When I was playing, I did not hit 57% of my shots to C; I always thought I needed to go closer to the lines and change directions because I felt like that's what the pros were doing. That's what 'offense' meant to me. I felt like I was losing matches because I couldn't hit the same offensive shots as many other players. I always thought my forehand needed to be bigger and do more damage to my opponent; it was like I was trying to play offense on every shot. **But now I see that I was losing matches because I couldn't hit clean enough, I couldn't stay neutral, and eventually, I'd leave a ball that was attackable for my equal. This helped me think of being 'neutral' as a form of offense in an overall gameplan**. Once I understood this, I started registering balls in my head as "C Balls" or "Non-C Balls," and I instantly started playing better. My head was clear; I knew I was playing pro-style tennis, which made me relax, and what's more, it was simple. Now I needed to hit all my groundstrokes cleaner and heavier, get my serve up into the 120 mph range, and effectively return 120 mph serves. This new understanding made things clear to me.

Whether it's a slice, approach shot, pass, flat, heavy, doesn't matter, hit it to C. C is where most points end. C is your opponent's backhand side. **Tennis is a C to C game.** It is the most valuable place to play shots on the court. It is, at the same time, offense, defense, and neutral. In short, it's always a good decision to go to C. And in a game of minimizing errors, C is the right answer for many reasons.

Make your opponent beat you with their backhand. Very few players have better backhands than forehands. He might get a rhythm with his backhand, but that's no big deal; players aren't trained to win with their backhands. They may be steady, but they aren't as dangerous from that wing as they are from their forehand. It's generally more surprising when a player hurts you with their backhand than with their forehand.

> *As an experiment, what would happen if you played an entire match where you tried to hit to your opponent's backhand as often as possible? It doesn't matter if that means you're hitting all your backhands down the line to a lefty backhand. You're still playing their weaker side, which is what the pros do. That should be your best strategy to win. Try it in a practice set, and see how it goes. Maybe we're making this game more complicated than it needs to be by trying to use different shot combinations and patterns in our matches when we could play more straightforward, basic strategies that are proven to be more effective.*

Thinking this way helped me relax mentally in both practices and matches. I was no longer trying to create offense with every shot. I didn't feel pressure to create angles when there were none to be had. I felt like all I had to do was hit each shot as clean as I could into B or C until a more obvious shot presented itself. I played with the expectation that only 10% of my shots throughout a match should land in A or D. I turned my practices into my partner and me with cones on B and C, trying to hit as big, heavy, clean, and deep as we could at either cone. We were developing our most massive neutral ball; a neutral ball is a shot that an opponent of your equal ability cannot reasonably play offense on. **When I'm 'neutral' in a point, I'm not trying to hurt my opponent so much as test him. Does he have the physical ability and the mental discipline to stay neutral with me?**

While drilling B&C this way, I was choosing which cone to aim at on each shot based on where the ball was coming from (angle of reception) and which direction my body was moving. **Hitting the ball in the direction I'm already moving gets more weight on my shot, improves my balance through the shot, and raises the quality of the ball off my racket.** I always want to hit the ball in the direction my body is moving. One out of every ten shots played on the ATP Tour goes into A&D

combined. Imagine that. That's why I want to spend a good portion of my practice time becoming as skilled as I can through B&C, where 90% of points are decided. Try charting it for yourself. Pick any match you want, record which zone every shot lands in, and see what you end up with. Sometimes charting matches is the best way to understand it and learn it for yourself. Watching so many matches like this made me really appreciate it, more so than playing ever did.

Watching and studying matches is a great way to improve without putting your body through practice's physical demands. In Anders Ericsson's book, "Peak: Secrets From the New Science of Expertise," he talks about the theory of 'chunking.' Chunking is essentially the ability to see common situations and predict the outcomes; Chess grandmasters are extraordinary at this. It's a critical element that separates them from the rest of the field. This skill helps them play chess as a series of moves that work together in combination, whereas novice players move their pieces as individuals with little regard for how one move affects their next. I have had a similar experience from watching matches; I know what shots players are most likely to hit based on where they are on the court, where their opponent is, and where the ball is. Then I study what's happening in different scoring situations and find patterns to what players are doing when they're in the different scenarios. Charting matches has dramatically helped my anticipation, which is a significant skill in our game. Watching matches is a major part of what I do with the professionals and top juniors that I work with.

Understanding this strategy will help you emphasize your shots' weight and cleanliness and help you recognize good and bad misses, along with good and bad decisions. To consistently win against your equal, you've got to be able to beat them through B&C. **You've got to be able to play consistent, aggressive tennis that**

applies pressure but doesn't take so much risk that you can't sustain it—controlled aggression. I can't think of a more aggressive, confident mentality than to think you can beat your opponent by hitting the ball to them, because that is to say you're better than them; you're not worried about them hurting you. This is a very different strategy and mindset than going on court and thinking you need to hit a winner or get your opponent on the dead run in two shots to win the point. Playing with these percentages as a guide tells your opponent that you don't need miracles to beat him, you're ready to beat him in the quarters this week, and first-round next week.

Playing this model makes matches simple because most of your gameplan stays the same no matter the opponent. There's no secret. You don't need to do a new version of XYZ with each new opponent. You need to figure out how you can get weak balls from him and where to serve him. If you made these decisions quicker, aka ball recognition, you could spend more time and energy getting into better hitting positions that allow you to hit heavier and heavier. **With a calmer mind, a heavier ball, and a more concrete game plan, you'll be a better player.**

It is statistically more common for a point to end through some sort of error by a player, while both players are in neutral positions than to see the point end with a great shot. The most errors come from Zone C. C is your opponent's backhand. That's why C is a great place to hit your shots no matter what position you're in on the court. When I call the players 'neutral', I mean that neither player had a massive advantage when the error was made and that both players are of relatively equal caliber. So if it's best to be neutral in a point, at least until an obviously offensive opportunity presents itself, then the question is, 'What's the best style of neutral to play?'

Should you play high and heavy like an Argentine or smooth and slow like an Indian? The truth is that you have to be able to play all styles, speeds, and strategies to beat your equal consistently. So what you should do is practice hitting the ball with topspin, slice, flat, while using ABCD to guide your shot selection and decision making. You need to be able to handle high heavy balls to your forehand and fast, low, flat balls to your forehand. That's why mastery is the goal. So don't worry too much about what type of ball you're hitting, practice them all, and figure out which one comes out of your racket best. Which one do you hit most naturally? Which one do you have the most control over? Find out if your flat backhand is your most effective, reliable backhand and then get good at that. If you can really control it, and you hit it consistently one foot over the net, that's ok- you just need excellent ball control to play with that little margin for error. Clearly, Argentines and Brits, Spaniards and Russians can be great players, so it's not so much their style or how they hit the ball that should be copied, but their strategy. And according to the method put forward in this book, most players are using the same basic design, ABCD, against each other, just with different ways of hitting the ball.

Different players should use the percentages differently. **The same information can mean different strategies depending on what the player's physical and mental strengths are.** In my experience, the best players align their game with their mentality and personality. They control their emotions and use them to their benefit in competition; McEnroe and Federer are different guys on court, but both act according to their personality and used their emotional strengths to fuel their game. You can't make McEnroe act like Federer, or vise versa. Reilly Opelka and Fabio Fognini are going to have vastly different game plans, but they're still playing within the same parameters of ABCD- Opelka may take more risk with his forehand and in his return games because he has that almost impenetrable serve. Opelka can afford to play lower percentage tennis because of his strengths, not just because his forehand is world-class. Every player has to find this symmetry on their own.

An excellent way to do this is to film your practices, looking for similar type balls that you consistently miss. Let's say you miss while on the run. Then practice working on balls while you're on the run. It's straightforward, like a doctor seeing a patient. Figure out what the illness is and prescribe the correct medication. If you're missing on the run, don't spend extra time serving. Spend time on the run and get better at it. **If you're a player who likes to move forward in the court and shorten points, spend your practice time transitioning forward. Look for balls in rallies that sit up and could be attacked. Don't worry if you're missing after 20 shots. If your game is to move forward, get great at that. Still spend some practice time building your shot tolerance, but not all of it. There is a time and place for it, but mentally think of it more as a conditioning drill than how you actually want to play in matches.**

Better players have better court sense, i.e., anticipation and feel for the ball, meaning they seem to make stretch volleys, tough passes, and good returns, so how do we make up for that? How do we get good at those tough shots? We've got to train our eyes to pick up on the flight of the ball better.

A good drill I do to work on the connection between the ball and my hand is I go out to the parking lot and hit with no net and no lines. My eyes judge where the net should be, and where the baselines would be, and I have a rally only using my feel for the game to let me know if I'm doing it well or not. Just focus on hitting the ball back to your partner. Find the rhythm. Don't worry about how heavy your ball is or how fast you're hitting. See how long you can go without missing. Your eyes will get tuned in to every aspect--speed, spin, depth, weight. Before you know it, you're hitting for an hour without missing. Getting in tune with the ball and your hand will help you develop the skills you need to make those tough passes or volleys that often determine big points in matches.

A few points decide matches against your equal, and very often, those points can hinge on difficult shots you rarely practice like half-volleys or squash shots. So practice making every shot, not being tentative, not just not-missing, practice getting in tune with the ball. See if you can be early to every shot, balanced through contact, with good racket head speed. See if you can do everything right on every shot because that's what the pros do. **You'll know when you get it right, and you'll feel the rhythm.**

Relax, You Know

A significant benefit of understanding the percentages and how they relate to your game is how this understanding relaxes your mind on court. You now know that a certain percentage of balls go into each zone. So any time your opponent hits a screamer into A, you know that only happens 3% of the time. Nothing to sweat over, let alone protect against or beat yourself up about. **The quicker you register shots like this, the faster you can reset and play the next point with no mental energy lost.** What if she is making a higher percentage of forehands into D than expected? You'll then notice that she's playing a higher percentage of balls to D than normal, and you'll understand how to defend against it. **Being aware and noticing what the trends are is the only way to successfully make adjustments mid-match.**

Mentally understanding what happens on the court can help you be more positive, or at least more mentally stable throughout the course of a match. You know that only 3% of passes get hit for outright winners, so instead of getting upset and telling yourself, 'This is why

I don't come to the net!', after you get passed, you can tell yourself, 'Alright, well that actually won't happen again, let's see what happens the next time she hits a forehand pass.' **Knowing the facts of what's happening during a match will spare you the overly dramatic moments that mostly sap your energy and help you stay focused on what matters.** How many people lose matches because they get so negative that they either end up physically drained or tank because they can't get over the two lucky shots their opponent hit? Getting passed outright by someone's backhand is like the net cord not going your way—you can't control it, and it probably won't happen often enough to matter, but the unknowing competitor will let that ruin their day.

Understanding what's going on on the court also helps players tactically. Most professional players go on the match court with gameplan A, B, and C as well as specific tactics based on their opponent that day. But most matches are won using a combination of strategies and some improvisation by the player at crucial times. Being able to make mid-match strategic adjustments is one factor that separates players of different levels and helps more physically 'average' players win consistently.

At every level of the game, there are players with seemingly no weapons who consistently win matches. This player is smart and great at recognizing what's going on during matches; they find your weaknesses and exploit them. They know how to turn things in their favor. To be smart, you have to be smart. You need to know what you can expect from yourself, what shots you can and cannot hit. **Being prepared is how you win.**

Having a strategy based on percentages and odds relaxes a player's mind because they know they will have a similar base game plan for every match as well as a clear idea of what their opponent may do. This is mostly applicable at the professional level where players do not have apparent weaknesses, and no pattern will guarantee a point won. **In practice, you develop new techniques, shots, strategies, and skills, but you keep it simple in matches. You don't clutter your brain with thoughts of implementing new tactics until you've got them down solid in practice.** If you agree with this, then practice time should be highly specific and applicable, a blend of fundamentals and specifics based on each player's needs.

TWO
WINNERS AND UNFORCED ERRORS

One of the most commonly talked about statistics in tennis is a player's winners to unforced errors ratio. It's important, but I think the way it's currently recorded is wrong and gives players and coaches a false sense of what really matters in tennis matches of equal players. In the rule book, a winner is a ball that lands in and bounces twice before the opponent touches it. An unforced error is a shot that is missed, that shouldn't have been. **Tennis against your equal requires a more refined understanding of winners and unforced errors, and the grey area in between those two.** I agree that tennis is a game of errors, but at the highest level or against your equal, I'd say they are rarely 'unforced.' My understanding of what winners and unforced errors are shapes how I think the game should be practiced and played.

I'll start with disproving the idea that you can simply look at the errors to winners ratio at the end of a match and fully understand what happened out there. Let's say you serve and volley behind a great kick serve out to the backhand of a righty on the add side and put a high forehand volley away cross-court that the returner doesn't even run for. Boom, that's a winner on the stat sheet. Now, imagine you are in the eighth ball of a rally through B&C, and you hit a screaming backhand down the line into A for a winner. Boom, another winner on the stat sheet. These two scenarios are not equal in my book. One is significantly more challenging to do than the other. One happens substantially more often than the other, but they are identical on the stat sheets, the way we have them working right now. Counting these two scenarios as the same skews the data that ends up on the stat sheet after the match, which gives people the wrong idea of what really happens in matches.

To me, a winner is a ball that bounces twice, against a 'ready' opponent. **There are about 4-8 winners per match at the ATP level in two out of three-set matches the way I think of them. A 'ready opponent' is in position to hit a balanced shot in reply to yours; imagine you are both neutral in the point. Hitting winners against a ready opponent is very difficult and should not be your strategy. Changing the way we understand and calculate winners and unforced errors is vital to how we play the game and practice it.** If we look at a recent Dimitrov match, for example, and see that in three sets against Thiem, he hit 46 winners, that means he must've been playing fantastic tennis! Nearly every point ended with Dimitrov ripping a winner! I doubt it.

What happens as a result of this winners number, though, is that players then go out to the practice court and try to figure out how they can hit 50 winners per match, because they just saw Dimitrov do it—and he did it against Thiem, so the college player needs to REALLY find a weapon if he wants to be a professional. Now the player will spend countless hours with his coaches creating drills, and scenarios, in the hopes that he'll be hitting more winners. Then he'll play practice sets and matches where he's looking to increase the number of winners he hits per match, and he'll either end up a god or a furious, tired, disheartened tennis player.

You need to have a weapon to be a professional, as well as to beat your equal consistently, but weapons are not necessarily 'winner generators.' The bottom line here is that looking for winners is a fool's errand, and changing your understanding of what a 'winner' is will change the way you practice and compete because it will change your strategy. Having a sound system and a theory of how to manage risk can help you win more matches, just like having a bigger forehand can. Truly both need to be developed as players work toward their potential.

Tennis is a game of errors. It's also a game that is most often won by the player who plays offense at the right times and in the right ways. Here's what registers to me as an unforced error and a forced error; **unforced errors are shots you miss or make the wrong decision on when you only have one option.** Every shot in tennis has to land inside the lines. When hitting a shot, the first thing in your mind should be, 'this ball will land inside the lines.' You do whatever it takes to get the ball in. So let's say you're on the dead run, 8 feet behind the baseline moving to your backhand side, you're opponent is still on his baseline, you're only viable option is to slice the ball back and let him have a potentially easy put-away ball on his next shot. That's ok, it happens, too good. If you go for a screaming backhand down the line winner, from this position, that's an unforced error. You only had one option, but you chose a less smart option. That's on you. To me, the big difference between forced and unforced errors is the decision the player made—whether he makes or misses the shot is less important. We can always control the decisions we make, but we can't always control our shots' outcome. If the player made the right decision, I leave it at that.

Now, let's imagine you get an inside out forehand, and you've registered that it's going to be in your strike zone, and you decide that you want to play it a bit more aggressively inside-in to catch your opponent off guard, fair enough. Take your shot, play to win. You have to. But now let's say you miss that shot, that's not an unforced error. It's just an error, a missed shot. Playing offense was the correct decision— we agreed on that already. You are forced to play offense against your equal, by the sheer fact that your opponent is your equal. A more accurate name for this type of shot would be an 'error while on offense' if you want to call it anything.

    The best players are looking to play offense, but not on every shot. If you agree that tennis's best strategy is to be offensive-minded, you also have to agree that with offense comes errors. Rarely can you play mistake-free offense, in any sport. But rarely can you win in any sport by simply not making errors. In my opinion, the two go hand-in-hand and thus need to be accepted, planned for, and not fretted over when they happen. **Unforced errors are bad decisions, not just missed shots.** If you have a couple options of shots you could hit, and you choose the hardest, riskiest one, whether you make or miss that shot it's still an unforced bad decision. You chose to go for it when you could've played it safer. Don't let yourself off the hook just because you made the shot. Always look at the decision you made and see if it was the right one.

    Against your equal, you've got to play offense to win. To me, that means that as you're playing the match, you are registering every single shot as either 'offense, neutral, or defense' and then hitting a shot in accordance with what you recognize as available in front of you. Sometimes you will get this wrong—you'll play neutral when you could have played offense, and you'll play defense when you could have played neutral, rarely will you play a match and make every decision, of the millions you have to make per match, precisely right. No worries, you're not alone.

    This is a grey area that's open to interpretation, but for

me, this is where intent comes into play. Judge yourself based on your decisions with each shot rather than the execution of each shot: intent and honesty. The player has to know what his intention is with every shot. Every missed shot is not an unforced error, sometimes you just miss a shot within your variance, it's not a big deal and it's not something to stress over on the stat sheet after matches.

Errors and winners are only discussed after the outcome; tennis strategy against your equal, should not be based on outcome. You have to pick a strategy, play it, and then make mid-match adjustments that no one can anticipate except the player. Figure out if the strategy was right or wrong after the match, when you rewatch the tape, and see what opportunities there were. Were you missing opportunities for offense? Were you forcing offense? You can look through all these moments in the match and decide how successful your strategy was, but it shouldn't be based on whether you made the shots or not. **I believe that once you get past the outcome and focus more on intent, you can play this game at a higher level.** You'll be playing at a higher level because you won't be attached to the outcome or as self-critical as you used to be before, during, and after matches. You will hopefully be a bit more calculated about the whole game, but that will help you balance the highs and lows of your game, as well as the mental highs and lows that come with competition in this sport.

THREE
SKILLING, NOT DRILLING

Tennis is a game of inches. Who will make the right decisions and have the most accuracy in the big moments? That's what many tournaments and matches boil down to. The hard part is that each match may come down to a different skillset: maybe it's going to be your volleys, or your ability to hit rally balls with depth, or your ability to take the ball early and take time away from your opponent. So how do you possibly prepare for all of it? You train your skills. We've talked about pro-level decision-making and risk management, now let's get into the physical side of how to grow our skill sets to their potential. Queue 'skilling.' Figure out a weakness or an area you'd like to work on in your game and work on that skill. Don't get caught up in how well you're doing the drill, or if it appears realistic or not, just isolate the skill, and rework it; use myelin.

A breakdown of what myelin is and how it works that helps me comes from Dan Coyle's book, "The Talent Code" and he writes:

'To sum up: it's time to rewrite the maxim that practice makes perfect. The truth is, practice makes myelin, and myelin makes perfect. And myelin operates by a few fundamental principles."

1. **The firing of the circuit is paramount**. Myelin is not built to respond to fond wishes or vague ideas or information that washes over us like a warm bath. The mechanism is built to respond to actions: the literal electrical impulses traveling down nerve fibers. It responds to urgent repetition.

2. **Myelin is universal.** One size fits all skills. Our myelin doesn't 'know' whether it's being used for playing shortstop or playing Schubert: regardless of its use, it grows according to the same rules. Myelin is meritocratic: circuits that fire get insulated. If you moved to China, your myelin would wrap fibers that help you learn to speak Mandarin. To put it another way, myelin doesn't care who you are—it cares what you do.

3. **Myelin wraps—it doesn't unwrap.** Like a highway-paving machine, myelination happens in one direction. Once a skill circuit is insulated, you can't un-insulate it (except through age or disease). That's why habits are hard to break. The only way to change them is to build new habits by repeating new behaviors—by myelinating new circuits.

4. **Age Matters**. In children, myelin arrives in a series of waves, some of them determined by genes, some dependent on activity. The waves last into our thirties, creating critical periods during which time the brain is extraordinarily receptive to learning new skills. Thereafter we continue to experience a net gain of myelin until around the age of fifty, where the balance tips toward loss...This is why the vast majority of world-class experts start young. Their genes do not change as they grow older, but their ability to build myelin does.'

Skilling, Not Drilling

Let's combine Coyle's theory of how to practice most efficiently with my view of what to practice in order to reach your potential and beat your equal in tennis.

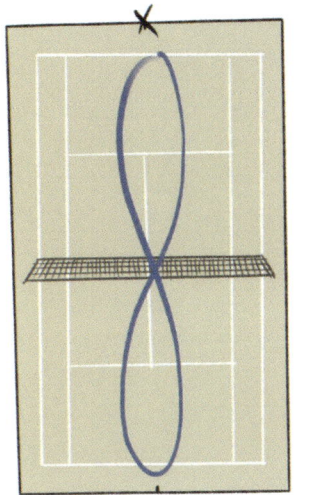

Say you want to work on taking the ball early; a drill you can do is, make one player stand on top of the baseline, while the player he's rallying with stands a bit farther back behind the baseline than he usually would. Now you can do B&C from this alignment, or any other drill. Mix up live ball hitting, with dead ball feeding where the player takes the ball early, and now you're doing it all.

Skilling requires the player to control their mind and emotions as much as it does their physical bodies. Building myelin is not easy, and sometimes the drills don't work out in action like they do on paper, so it can be challenging for the players to stay focused on learning the skill, but that practice of staying focused is valuable as well. This is just like pushing the threshold, a topic I cover later in the book, sometimes you're pushing the threshold of how long you can hold off frustration—a tremendous skill to have as a tennis player. **There are mental skills that come into play when trying to win a tennis match against your equal; ignoring these skills during practice will leave you consistently coming up short.**

Looking

Being able to dictate how points are played in your matches is a crucial skill; the player who dictates most often will win most often. **Federer can create offense with shots that the #100 player in the world would be neutral on, and that's why Federer will consistently**

win against him. Yes, there are talent and skill differences between the two players, but there are also recognition differences. Federer sees a moment in the ball's flight path that may offer him a chance at offense, while the #100 player doesn't see it or isn't skilled enough to act on it.

Reading the flight of the ball and knowing what opportunities it presents is a skill I call, "Looking." So often in 50/50 match ups, when there's no 'obvious' ball to attack on, it's the player with a slightly better eye who can hit a couple good, difficult shots in important scoring situations in the match who will win.

To work on this skill, I love doing a drill where two players are hitting through B&C, looking to take a ball to A&D. In this instance, the coach and player are not overly concerned with the player's shot being in, but instead, they're focused on not missing an opportunity to go to A&D. This is where the player and coach must know each other well because not all players think offensively on the same balls. Training yourself to look for Attackable balls will pay off when you play your equal, and opportunities are not obvious.

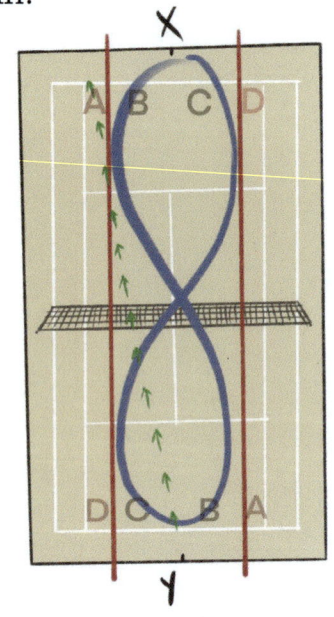

When the coach knows the player well enough, he can help the player take advantage of weaker balls and see the opportunity in weaker balls that the player may not see. It's difficult to tell when and how 'looking' will pay dividends, but it does. If it's not a physical skill that decides who wins and loses a match, then it's intangibles like making the right play at the right time, and that's what you're practicing while you work on looking.

When I'm working on looking with a player, it has almost nothing to do with technique; we are past that and into watching the flight of the ball. Now we're talking about where the ball was on your body when you hit it, 'Was it in your strike zone?' 'Was your body set?' And so you break down where you typically like to make contact, given the ball you're working on, and that helps you know when you should pull the trigger on that shot. You begin to make your decision of where to hit the shot based on your skill at hitting the ball while it's at that certain height on your body. Now you know how you hit that shot, and what characteristics you're looking for in the ball's flight path to execute it. You learn to make decisions based on the type of ball your opponent gives you, and not just on 'feel.'

A 'looking' drill I love to do for developing a weapon from your forehand side is I'll have two players rallying crosscourt, and set up two cones somewhere down the line,

and somewhere angled crosscourt. The player on one side is simply the 'hitter' while the other player tries to get five forehands through each window created by the cones. You can do the same drill for forehand inside out or inside in, and backhand down the line and cross-court. Using the window is a visual tool that trains the player's eye to see the court in a way that aiming for cones doesn't.

Four
Training the Minimums

Playing the minimums is a strategy that gets players to play as offensively as possible with as much margin as possible. Players must have a solid, honest understanding of their variance and skill level and a proper mental representation of the situation they're in on court to be able to play the minimums to the best of their abilities. Once you've got an understanding of the shots you can and cannot hit, you can talk about what your options were on each shot during practice, or when rewatching matches. I think it's crucial players use the percentages of ABCD as a guide, and then tailor it for their individual style and skill-set.

Training isn't always about doing it better. Your forehand doesn't need to get faster every practice. Your forehand needs to be consistently able to execute shots at the same level. Some practices should be about being as good as you were yesterday. See if you can maintain a certain level of play over a certain number of hours; many matches are decided by which player can play at a higher level for a longer time. That's why the Big 3 win so many matches at the Grand Slams; almost inevitably, the lower-ranked players can't maintain the level needed to succeed in best out of five sets, allowing the Big 3 to prevail. In my opinion, we should be training with this in mind. We need to know that we can execute certain shots or specific patterns so that we feel confident about our level. That way, we can make a specific gameplan and have confidence in our abilities to execute.

Let's say A,B,C,D percentages are 'right' as guidelines for a top-level player to play by. Now how do we master it? Playing by the percentages gets players to 'play the minimum,' but it doesn't teach them how to manage risk or make adjustments to their risk-taking tendencies. Understanding and being able to adjust the amount of risk you take during a match is the goal. **Only hitting 90% of your shots through B&C won't win you matches; managing risk wins you matches. That's why it's more important to understand what playing the minimums means. That way, you can apply it in different scenarios, and not just play through B&C like a robot.**

For example, Nakashima should use his flat backhand down the line when he sees the opportunity; he's absolutely money with it. I wouldn't recommend many players use their backhand down the line as a way to attack their opponent, but it's not a risk for Brandon the way it is for other players. I'd rather him hit a flat backhand down the line into A, then take an inside-in forehand to A. He's better with his backhand. And that's built into our gameplan and his mindset when playing matches. It's knowing yourself as the player and your player as the coach that becomes crucial in deciding what playing the minimums really means for each player. Watching film is a large part of what I do with the players I work with so that we can both watch the points unemotionally and see what options the player truly had. Typically we're less involved with the match when watching after-the-fact versus while we're playing, and we can see opportunities on film that we didn't see live.

Applying The Minimums

Time and again, you'll see some of the world's best players missing backhand passing shots that you'd never expect them to miss; this is a key area I have my players build their gameplan around no matter how often they come to the net in matches. The takeaway is, 'when you're forced to approach, and you can hit your approach anywhere, play it to the opponent's backhand.' This is strategically playing the minimums because it's your highest percent chance of winning the point, no matter how good of an approach shot you hit. You will win 78% of points where your opponent hits a backhand pass, and 56% of points where your opponent hits a forehand pass; so choose to play the backhand pass, and you're playing the minimums by taking the 78% chance of winning. It's not about approaching down the line or cross-court, it's about what side you approach against. Don't worry about what angles he may or may not be able to hit. Pick to approach the more limited side, and you're playing the minimums simultaneously.

Another example of playing the minimums, let's say you serve slice wide on the even side. Your opponent leaves an attackable return in the middle of the court. You've got his backhand side wide open. If you hit your shot into C you'll either hit a winner or he'll be stretched out on the run to his backhand. The player who truly plays the minimums will play that ball with enough speed and depth into C and follow the shot forward for a probable put-away volley—this is right because they played the safest amount of offense that still keeps them on offense. The player who doesn't understand the minimums, or has a flawed mental representation of the situation, may over hit this put-away shot, choosing excess speed, depth, angle, etc. Even if you hit this ball for a winner, it still is not playing the minimums; base your play on the decisions you make, not the outcomes. It's thinking this way in practice and matches that eventually pays off by turning into habits.

Mental Representations

Frequently players struggle with the finishing ball in a point, junior players especially, and so they spend hours practicing the actual shot. But the shot is easy—we all know it. In addition to practicing the shot, I'd challenge the player to think of what his mental representation is of that situation. What do you see when you have the inside out forehand I described above? Do you see yourself hitting a winner, or moving forward and knocking off a volley after your opponent's backhand pass? The best players see themselves hitting a volley off their opponent's backhand pass; they want the opponent to hit an on the run backhand pass. They anticipate playing the point all the way through, rather than imagining that they may hit a forehand inside out winner. Their idea of how the situation should play out is what helps them stay calm and execute the shot.

Think about Rafa Nadal when he first came onto the ATP tennis scene—he was a physical specimen, he was a battler. He was the last guy anyone wanted to play on clay because his tenacious mentality and playing style were perfect for clay. He won the French Open the first time he played it. But he was not the same player on the grass at Wimbledon. Initially his game didn't translate to the quicker, low-bouncing surface that allowed opponents to shorten points. Many people in the tennis world wrote Nadal off as a great clay court player but a guy who's game may never transfer to other surfaces. At the time, his game was limited and his skill set didn't look like it would be able to change. But Nadal wanted to be one of the greatest players, which meant he had to learn to win on grass.

I'm sure he made some technical changes, but mostly his mental representation of how to win on grass changed. He began seeing himself setting up points so that he could gain control in the first few shots; he started to see himself winning points at the net. He understood that he couldn't use his defensive skills as much on grass as he could on clay, and he adjusted. Nadal did not simply keep playing the same strategies on grass that helped him win on clay, he adapted his skills to the new requirements the grass imposes on all players. Only the people on his team know how much tinkering he did with his grass-court game before he was finally able to win Wimbledon, but the process of changing his mental representation of his own game on grass was most likely a large contributor to his success.

When coaches talked to me about managing risk I often felt like they were asking me to play offense on every shot, without missing. I was suffocated by pressure not to miss. I didn't have the proper mental representation for what they were asking me to do. Even if I had the skills to do what they suggested, I didn't have the understanding. It's especially important that coaches and players explain what they both envision while working on a particular area of the player's game before they go about trying to actually do it in practice and matches. While talking about the chaos of a professional soccer match, Ericsson writes,

> *"To those who know and love the game, however, and particularly to those who play the game well, this chaos is no chaos at all. It is all a beautifully nuanced and constantly shifting pattern created as the players move in response to the ball and the movements of the other players. The best players recognize and respond to the patterns almost instantaneously, taking advantage of weaknesses or openings as soon as they appear."*

Certain players are able to stand out in soccer and make great plays because they have a better understanding of what's really going on during play. They know where their teammates and opponents are on the field, and they use all of the players like pieces on a chess board. Ericsson writes, "**the relationship between skill and mental representations is a virtuous circle: the more skilled you become, the better your mental representations are, and the better your mental representations are, the more effectively you can practice to hone your skill.**" Again, pointing out that having an accurate and in-depth mental representation of what you're trying to do on the tennis court will dramatically increase the rate at which you improve. Having a clear mental representation of what playing the minimums means for your game, in all scenarios on court and scoring situations will help you master the concept.

Drilling the Minimums

Practice time needs to be specific. In my experience, the strategic side of tennis, and the mental understanding of how to adjust strategies is completely under-practiced. Players should spend a large part of their practice time playing through different scoring situations and talking with their coaches about what their options are; this type of practice will translate into more wins, and it will create players that are capable of adapting and problem-solving which is hugely important for their growth and success as tennis players. I use two main ways of coaching the minimums, both get at different mentalities but get the same idea across.

My favorite way to practice this is to put up the cones on B&C and play points aiming for either cone on every shot. All the regular rules of tennis apply, but players only win points when they hit a cone. First player to hit 5 cones wins. Or you can play regular singles points, first player to 10 points wins but if you hit a cone the game is instantly over. Hitting a cone is like catching the Golden Snitch in Quidditch.

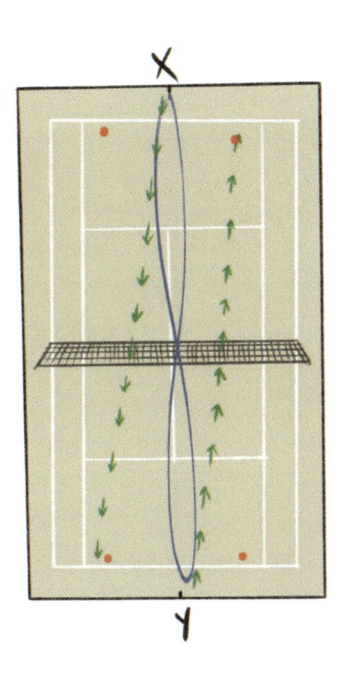

This keeps players engaged because it's the normal court and rules that they have to compete on, and it allows them to make adjustments that are realistic and instantly applicable to match play. Players score points when they hit a cone, which gets competitive. And from the coach's perspective this drill helps because I know that with every shot the player is supposed to be aiming at a cone, so I can get a great idea of their variance and they can't tell me they were trying to do something else, because the whole point of the game is to hit a cone. It gets rid of all confusion. If they hit a sweet angle forehand winner cross, they lost sight of what the drill is; it's not a fantastic shot, it's a lack of focus and understanding.

The second way I teach this strategy is to let players play singles on the full doubles court. This way works well because players feel they have more room for error, as well as less need to go for the new A and D. Most times, the players will hardly use the alleys, but they'll feel less pressure, just knowing that the alleys are in. With extra room, the alleys, and the bigger court- keeping their opponent honest- players can play as aggressively as they like, and they'll probably play mostly in the singles court. Having the alleys in makes their opponent's court bigger and harder to cover. Both of these realities relax the player which helps them see that they don't need to force shots or force offense.

I like these variations because each variation's mentality is different, and not all players will 'click' with the same drill. The different mentalities are also essential to use given the player's mood or mindset. If they struggle with playing to B&C, open up the doubles alleys and watch the change that happens in the player.

It's common for tennis players to work on their serve and forehand when trying to 'get to the next level,' 'I need to have weapons' is a phrase I've heard a lot.

Having weapons that hit winners is not the only way to play offense against your equal or better; being a good thinker can get you into offensive situations with exactly the weapons you have now.

In fact, I'd say trying to develop a serve that hits more aces and a forehand that hits more winners is the hardest way to try and win more matches. Also, by going for more on your first serves and forehands, you're choosing to play lower percentage tennis, which is typically not sustainable against your equal or better players.

I suggest that players work on their ball striking ability; earn yourself the right to be in rallies with better players than you. **Use the quality of your ball to get you offensive opportunities, and then take those when they come.** Think of Nalbandian or Baghdatis— they don't have obvious weapons against the other top players, but they are great ball strikers. Over the course of a match, they wear opponents down physically and mentally.

Futures guys should live on B&C, not because they can't do anything else, but because it's what works. If you hit the ball well, direct 60% of your shots through C or B against lefties. This is your best strategy at beating Challenger guys. Futures guys generally lack the control to win through A&D—rarely does anyone at any level, by the way. Again, generally speaking, Futures guys think that the difference between them and Challenger guys is that Challenger guys can hit winners from the baseline and finish points on almost any ball, and that's not necessarily true. **Challenger level players have better mental representations of what's needed to win a given match, and they have greater command of the skills required to execute. They do to Futures guys what ATP guys do to them.**

Players looking to add offense to their games would get there quicker and safer if they spent time working on their ball striking ability—a cleaner, heavier ball yields more short balls with less risk than just aiming at A&D more frequently. A heavier ball, along with a clear mental representation of why you're using one strategy over another, will change the type of player you are. The poster boy for this model today is Dominic Thiem. His most obvious plan of attack is to bludgeon the ball through B&C and beat his opponents with his weight of shot. Eventually, against most players in the world, his opponent will mishit a shot, and Thiem will take that opportunity to take control of the point and finish it. When he does this well, he's one of the best players in the world.

Being confident in your ability to play through B&C is a pure form of offense; it is true confidence when you hit your shots to your opponent and still feel that they can't beat you. **I think aiming at the B&C cones is the best general practice drill because it allows for decision making and ball recognition, while playing the same strategies as the top pros.** The most significant difference between Futures and ATP players is their ability to exist inside B&C. Drill B&C as big and heavy as you possibly can, and you'll be playing the minimums as aggressively as possible, and that's a real, calculated form of offense.

FIVE INDULGENCES

    Indulgences are thoughts or actions that serve no purpose in your goal of reaching your potential. They take you farther away from reaching your potential, you know they do, and yet you give into them anyway. Pretending you'll never win a big match again after a tough loss, that's an indulgence. Telling everyone at the club how bad your backhand is, that's an indulgence. Thinking you don't need to train with purpose because you won the last tournament you played, indulgence. **Figuring out what your indulgences are and cutting them out of your mental diet is key to growth.**

    Indulgences happen to everyone. **My goal is to limit how much they affect my level of play during a match.** Pro players get mad, and they may say things like, 'F*%k, I can't miss that,' after an easy miss. They might even crack a racket or two. But they're able to get over that initial anger or frustration and quickly get back to their normal physical and mental level so that they can continue trying to win the match.

    I'd say there is a direct correlation between how much

better you are than your opponent and how much you can allow indulgences to affect you without affecting the outcome of the match, which means that ATP level players can afford more indulgences against a Futures level player than they can against another ATP level opponent. Even though you may win the match, giving in to the indulgence of the day is still a negative. Just like winners and unforced errors, the decision you make is more important than the outcome of it. Learning to fight your indulgences is the goal, not winning despite yourself.

I'd say for the best players in the world it's about more than just controlling your reaction to the negative, it's about creating the positive. Finding the good things to focus on that make you want to play well and train hard. I call those things 'motivators.' They can be a goal you use to challenge yourself, or a thought of pushing yourself past a mental level you are used to performing at. The world's best are experts at this. I didn't understand how to balance dealing with indulgences and creating motivators until I was out of college.

A great way to get better at dealing with things that don't go your way on court is to stop looking for them. Look for the good stuff. The things you're doing right and want to get better at. It doesn't always work, it's difficult to only think about things this way, but it is another way to minimize the effect your indulgences have on you.

Minimizing the effect your indulgences have on you is a key area of your game that can separate you from the players that are currently your equal. Matches of equal opponents are often decided by a few points, so those three games you played out of anger definitely could've decided the match, let alone just a few angry points. Always keep in mind that the goal of all the training and thinking you do about your game is to get as close to your potential as you can. **Improvement has to be the primary goal**. Dealing with your indulgences is just as important as working out. You don't know when, where, why or how, but those extra sprints will pay off, just as that self-talk will.

The goal is to align as many of your thoughts and actions that relate to tennis with your overall goal of improvement. You don't want to workout hard and then eat junk food; workout hard and eat right and get the rewards. They're two parts of being your best, no difference. It's the same thing with your thoughts. If you want to be nails in big moments, then think that you're nails in big moments, not that you always choke in big moments. Do your best to have your thoughts supporting your game while you're out there on court.

Our lives as tennis players are highly repetitive: wake up early, warm-up, practice, stretch, lunch, chill, practice, workout, stretch, sleep, repeat. So eventually, we build habits. Habits can be thought patterns as well as physical actions. **We've got to consciously decide what we think as well as what we do; replacing our negative indulgences with motivators until they become habits.** In moments of weakness, we fall back on our habits, no matter what they are, so if we can make our habits as productive as possible, we'll be thankful. This is the same theory as spending practice time aiming for the baseline; we're trying to build the physical habit of hitting the ball deep in the court. Mentally we want to build the habit of making our thoughts as productive as possible.

Indulgences Stifle Growth

One of the main drawbacks of allowing negative indulgences on court with you is how much work they prevent you from getting done. Let's say you're pissed that you're not hitting your backhand well, and you need to figure it out and work on it. Fair enough. But now how much of the remaining practice time is eaten up by more indulgences like throwing your racket or hitting balls out of frustration, or not moving at full speed anymore because you're overwhelmed by anger? This is where indulgences do the most damage. They infect your brain, and then they take over your practice session. Instead of calmly thinking about your backhand and how to work on it, or simply moving on and hitting some volleys to get the backhand issues out of your head, many players wallow in the anger or frustration and ruin their entire practice. To me, this is where players lose me. If you're really trying to reach your potential, you wouldn't allow this to happen. You simply wouldn't allow yourself to waste days. This is why being aware of yourself—your thoughts and actions—can help you mature and tremendously help your game. Juniors with a more 'professional' head could be professional players.

When this happened to me, I would always try to replace the thought once I recognized it and couldn't figure it out. So, let's say I can't get the timing of my footwork when I'm pulled wide to the forehand side- once I think about what the footwork is, and how I should time it, I'll try it again. If I can't get it figured out, I'm going to move on and maybe I'll come back to the running forehand in 30 minutes. I may want to stay working on my forehand, but I decided before practice began that if I ran into a problem like this, I'd move on and come back to it. **I would actually decide how I was going to act on court, while I was off court relaxing.** I did this because I'm more logical when I'm off court; on-court me can be a psycho and prevent me from having a productive practice session. This strategy helped me gain back some of the time I was essentially wasting by being mad, or frustrated. I know there is work to be done in my game, and I want to spend the necessary time it takes as productively as possible, that's how I got to think this way.

This idea of deciding how I want to be in the moment before I got put in the moment is how I started to really make improvements in my game. I finally understood what the most productive version of myself was, and then all I had to do was have the discipline and desire to stick with it. For me, it was very hard to get past some of my indulgences; I had been ingraining them into my way of being for years. It took serious thought to change some of my habits. But that is the cool part. That is the part where you feel yourself becoming your potential. That, to me, is bigger than all but a few of my on court victories. **Getting control over your mind and body, and then harnessing that towards the path you want, that's what it's really about in my opinion. That's what sports can teach us.**

Indulgences are different from impulse reactions like a big 'c'mon' after bombing an ace, or a smashed racket after getting broken at 3-3 in the third. Those types of reactions are not what worry me, I'm fine with those. You've got to be a competitor, and you've got to let your emotions out when you feel you need to; but why not have them be as constructive as possible?

We can create mental representations of how we act on court, and how we carry ourselves through certain moments. **Control your emotions and change your impulses by thinking about how you want to be on court before you get out there**. The opening lines of Brad Gilbert's world-renowned book, "Winning Ugly", read:

'One of the first lessons I learned when I turned pro in 1982 was how much of an edge could be gained before the match even got started. It became obvious to me that for the best players in the world their match had begun a long time before the first serve. They came ready to play and wanted to grab me by the throat as soon as they could.'

Do you want to be saying 'c'mon'? Do you want to be placid and emotionless? Whatever and however you want to be, think about it, and then practice being that way. Understanding what indulgences are and aren't helps you decide what you really need to focus on in practice and what you don't. Later in the book, Gilbert writes,

'The smart ones {other players} were consciously and subconsciously reviewing information about the opponent ahead of them as soon as they knew who that player was. The process began hours before the match. The smart players wanted to seek and seize advantage as early as possible. And they wanted to do it in as many ways as possible. For them, one of the big opportunities was good mental preparation. And that means early mental preparation.'

Self-defeating dialogue that continues for games after you missed 'the easiest volley of all time' is an indulgence. Rarely does dragging that on make anyone play better. You can't afford to waste energy like that against your equal. It's hard to change our habits, but overlooking any poor habits is an indulgence. And indulgences are self-allowed once we become aware of them; so be firm with yourself. Sometimes you've got to look at the entire situation, like Gilbert explains, and adapt yourself and your game to hold up against the toughest competition you can find. **Every part of your game, including the mental side, is up for tweaking when improvement is your goal**.

For example, let me explain my time working with a high-level junior who was ready to start playing Futures. He is a great player with a big tennis body, an elastic arm and ticking time-bomb for a brain. He had a habit of negatively acting out during matches once things started going against him. He'd cheat, call the trainer, trash talk the opponent, whatever he could do to a) tell everyone watching how hard he was trying, and b) take all the responsibility for his being down in the score off of himself and put it on something else. It wasn't the pressure of winning and losing that he couldn't handle, he loves winning and he's played tennis his whole life; he's used to it. To me, it was something deeper than that. Let's assume it's not the pressure of winning and losing that sends his head into the gutter, and let's look for something else.

For me, I think it is the reality that he did not prepare for the match in the ways he knew he was supposed to. It could be different every time, but maybe he didn't eat enough for breakfast, maybe he cut the warm up short, maybe he didn't do his visualization exercises; it doesn't matter what actually set him off for the day, it matters that he told himself he'd prepare as best he could, he had a plan of how to do it and then he didn't do it. He didn't do the actions that he said he would. And he was fine with that until he started losing.

When the match started going against him he'd get angry and sad that it was happening to him, and he knew it was all on him. He knew that it wasn't his coach, or the old umpire, or the bad bounces, it was his own decision not to hold himself accountable. He indulged in the thought that whatever he had done to prepare was 'enough' even though he knew it wasn't. Figuring this out gave him all the information to improve and reach his potential. Understanding that he needed to control his approach to the game changed the way he competed and played more than anything we worked on on court. But it takes constant, indefatigable self-control to do all the things we say we want to do. And if you can't do that, I don't think you'll reach your potential. And that's really all there is to go after in sports, you're potential. No comparisons, just what you can be.

Just as honesty is important when training B&C, because it gives your coach the true insight he needs after you hit a shot, 'did you mean to go there?' - that question needs to be asked and answered honestly. The same is true with indulgences. I often asked the junior I mentioned above, 'Did you prepare fully in the way we talk about preparing?' Often, he would tell me that he did prepare properly, but he wasn't being honest with himself or me. He was stuck in his indulgences— doing things the same way he always had. I think the only way to actually change your habits, or indulgences, is to want to do it badly enough that you stick with it. We all have heard it takes X number of days to change a habit, or you can use this or that technique, but really you're either going to do it or you're not. Be honest about your intentions and your effort, and you'll get it done.

SIX
REALISTIC WAYS TO TRAIN

A match of equal players comes down to a combination of decision making and shot-making; some matches are decided by a couple miraculous shots at key moments, and others by solid decision making over the span of the entire match. Typically the most important matches of our careers come against opponent's who are our equal, where decision making will probably determine the outcome, but how often do we practice our decision making and our understanding of risk?

For example, on an important point do we know what types of shots we want to take our chances with? Do we know statistically what helps us win matches more often, or are we still making decisions based on 'feel'? Should we take our backhand down the line here, or cross and give the risk back to our opponent? To me, winning tennis matches is like investing money. You have to choose if you want to put money in risky stocks that offer bigger returns, or if you want to take the sure thing and slowly build up. **The best players can do both, they under-**

stand how and when to do both, and they make the right decision when the time comes to choose.

Sometimes there are BIG points that you can point to as the deciding factor in the outcome of a match, but there are also thousands of tiny decisions in a match that players have to make—and what I'm saying is 'what if we made those decisions better?' We may win matches handily that used to come down to one BIG moment. This is why my practices are set up around ball recognition and in the parts of the court where most points happen. **My theory is that if you make the smaller decisions better, you can win more matches.**

Get on the Offense

I operate with the belief that it's better to be on offense than defense--I want the outcome of the point and match to be on me. My goal as a player is to play the safest amount of offense I can for the most amount of time possible; sometimes that may mean staying neutral. In football, for example, I'd rather my team have the ball; there's minimal damage that can be done if my team has the ball, even if we don't score. It's much less likely that the defense creates a turnover and scores off it than if they would just score normally on offense. In fact, according to this data, in 2013 a defensive touchdown occurred once every other game on average. That's about 1 out of 266 plays[1]. That's why, in general, in any sport, playing offense is a more successful strategy than playing defense.

In tennis, as you go up in levels, you've got to be able to play offense against better players with the same percentages and margins for error that you used at lower levels. This means you've got to be able to stay neutral against the better players until you get an attackable ball from them. **Stay neutral until you get a ball you like.**

---

[1] "NFL Team Defensive Touchdowns per Game." NFL Football Stats - NFL Team Defensive Touchdowns per Game on TeamRankings.com, www.teamrankings.com/nfl/stat/defensive-touchdowns-per-game.

You do this by building up your weight of shot and the cleanliness of the ball coming out of your racket. It's nearly impossible to beat someone who hits a heavier ball than you because you know that if rallies stay neutral, you'll either miss or leave a short ball before they do. In this matchup, you're forced to play low percentage tennis; and low percentage tennis typically results in losses. Hitting a good enough quality ball to stay neutral against your equal is the most important part of winning tennis matches. Strategy comes next.

Try playing sets with rules as to how you will take risks. For example, 'I'll take risks with my backhand cross court, second serve returns, and my forehand down the line.' In this situation, you'll be clear that shots other than what you decided to work on get played into B&C, and you won't fall for the trap of trying to do more with shots that you shouldn't. Using rules like this in practice help you figure out what your weapons are, and how to use them.

So let's go on the hunt for better ways to train than what's generally accepted in the sport right now. Depth of shot is the most important factor when playing your equal, where balls that land short all but certainly mean the end of the point. So if depth is key, how do we work on it? Certainly not by training ourselves to make our shots land around the service line.

We spend years training ourselves on how to put the ball into a spot on the court that makes it easy for our opponent to hit it back to us. That is the opposite of what we want to do in matches. So what's the deal? **Rallying is valuable and necessary, but winning is more important.** Learning to hit the ball deep goes hand-in-hand with missing long, but that doesn't matter as much when you understand that you're learning. You're learning how to hit the ball deeper by firing the neural pathways that make the ball travel deeper. **'In' and 'out' have no pur-**

pose in this type of practice, the baseline is merely a guideline of where you want the ball to land based on the realities of tennis. Refining the skills of an elite professional athlete is all about myelin and making sure that every repetition of their practice has a purpose that results in them winning more matches.

In a match, it's time to compete and trust our game plan and habits. For a pro or high-level player, a percentage of training time should be spent hitting the ball with no consequences, meaning no lines, and then transition into having the standard lines on the court count as 'in' and 'out'. **We've got to give the athlete time to understand their swing and feel like they can experiment with it, and that's typically done best when you take away the feeling of failure and 'missing.'**

We can't play offense on every shot in a match. A large percentage of shots when playing against your equal are played with the intent of staying neutral. The best way to stay neutral is to hit as high-quality a ball as you can at your opponent's weaker side. It's something I've observed at every level--the better players hit a higher quality, 'cleaner' ball than the players they consistently beat. A clean, well-hit ball flies through the air straight. You can almost read the logo on the ball as it spins on its way back and forth between the players. It makes a crisp, solid sound when you make clean contact on a shot, and it goes off your racket easily, with seemingly little effort. It's all about timing.

Watch two Top 100 pros practice live, and you'll see what I'm talking about. Brandon Nakashima, although ranked #220 in the ATP Singles rankings, hits the ball as clean as most players in the Top 100. The quality of his ball is one of our biggest weapons when putting together a game plan for his matches; I may tell him, 'rely on the consistent weight and depth of your shot to keep you in control of the points.' Our strategy against many players was to bully them with the weight of Brandon's 'neutral' ball, until they either left a ball short that was attackable for Brandon, or they got impatient and decided to take a low percentage shot. Obviously we had specifics for each opponent that I won't share, but the overall game plan is typically very similar from match to match. In no way does that mean Brandon is waiting for them to miss or playing tentatively. I'd say it's almost the opposite. I'm telling him, 'hit as big as you can--right at the guy; build through B&C while looking for an opportunity to play offense.' **Feeling like you don't need to do anything special to beat your opponent is the ultimate form of offense and confidence.**

Hit Cleaner

There are many ways to try and hit the ball cleaner, but I'll avoid mentioning techniques because I believe it's overplayed. Every pro has a different technique, but a couple key components exist in nearly every top pros biomechanics. Although adjusting a player's technique is legitimate, too many coaches pick on technique because it's easy to convince players that they're just one minor or major change away from that next higher level. I believe a lot of coaches pass along cliches that their coaches told them; it's a never-ending cycle of bad information being passed down from generation to generation. Working on technique also eats up a ton of practice time, which is ideal for the uninterested coach. Look at the ATP Top 100 players and you'll see 100 different techniques on every stroke; the closest two techniques would be Federer and Dimitrov, and just looking like Federer hasn't gotten Dimitrov any Slams yet.

Hitting the ball cleaner comes from being in better control of all the factors that go into a shot; speed, spin, depth, angle, body positioning etc.

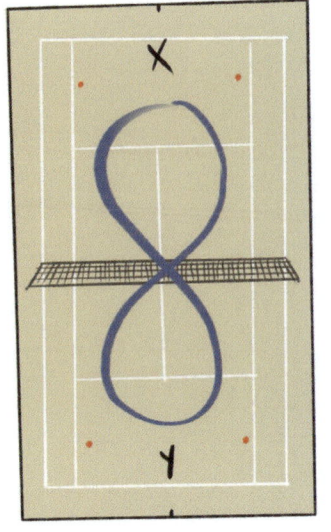

So to control all these factors we slow everything down. We try to master all these aspects. We make the court smaller and try to be as precise as possible; our mind is focused on striking the ball well. As the player's skill level increases, we make the court bigger. Eventually, we can ask players to hit on a court bigger than the normal singles court that they'll be playing matches on.

Adjusting the size of the court challenges their ball-control, and helps them hone that skill. Once the players are striking the ball cleaner, you can start working on strategy and decision-making. Everyone has weapons at the top levels, but it's the player who can control them and choose the most ideal time for using them who usually wins.

We have to assume top pros do everything on purpose, from how they move around the court to the shots they choose to hit. Otherwise, we're just calling them talented, and I don't believe the top players are just 'talented.' Skills can be learned. Many pro players, even those with a few ATP points, could become Top 100 pros with the right training. Top pros have better control over the variables that go into being good tennis players than the rest of us, likely because they worked harder and smarter than the rest of us while on court.

This is why we've got to make the court whatever size is necessary for the player to be in total control of all aspects. We want to feel like we're playing mini tennis. Staying in this control mode helps train our brains to know that we have to be able to build and win point after point against our equal, whereas when the factors aren't controlled, there are one-off winners we can hit to win points—reinforcing bad habits and thought processes. Looking for winners is not a strategy we can build a career on. **Having the ability to stay neutral with anyone in the world is a skill set you can create a career on. You need the ability to stay neutral long enough for your opponent to hit a shot that you can play offense on. Neutral, while looking for offense. That's the way. Whoever can stay neutral on harder shots typically wins the match.**

Inside this controllable setting, you can truly choose where and how to hit your shots, giving the player full responsibility for what happens, just as we give to the pros. Now we can add movement patterns and shot patterns that are useful in winning points against your equal.

You can put one guy hitting inside out forehands into C, and the other guy dealing with it and returning backhands into C, when the FH guy goes to D, the point starts. Any combination of drills like that help the player learn to hit the ball cleaner and with more accuracy. Drills like this need to be understood by the player because they are very mental; the player has to see the value in hitting clean balls. When he's able to do these drills at the required level, make the court bigger--challenging the player again.

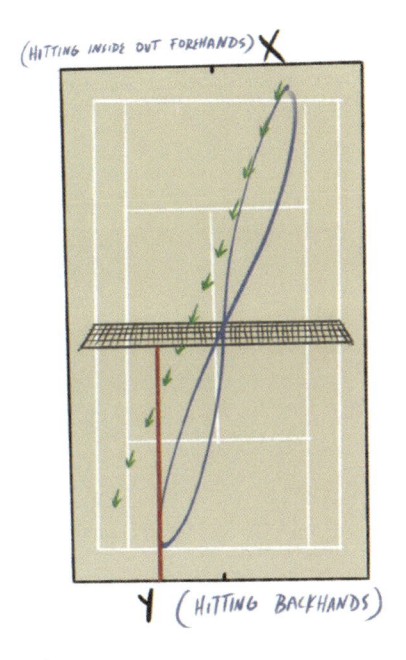

As we go up in levels, the players hit every ball faster, cleaner, deeper, and heavier than we're used to. So how do we deal with it and make ourselves able to not only stay neutral at this new level but to be better than the others who've already been up here? We've got to let go of 'in' and 'out' again because when we're learning a new skill, we don't have time to have our progress halted because of frustration over 'missing.' Players waste time being frustrated in practice because they're not focused on learning the new skill; they're focused on how this and that shot would've worked in a match. Practice is neither the time nor the place for that mindset.

One thing I do with my players is put the cones up at B&C and have them absolutely crush the ball if they can. This drill is a simple match strategy, and a realistic practice situation. If the players can find a rhythm and work up to a higher pace than they're used to, their body and eyes are getting used to responding to the type of ball they'll see at the higher levels. Again, I don't start with technique, I start with the mind, if we show the player a new speed and pace, with time they should be able to adjust. If they don't, then look at the technique. It's ok if the rallies aren't long at this speed; this drill is like going for your three rep max in the gym. Players gain confidence from making this drill work, as it should be challenging at the beginning. They are also firing the neural pathways that they need to play at this level; all of these drills and theories for realistic training can be traced back to the brain. Myelin. That's what it's about.

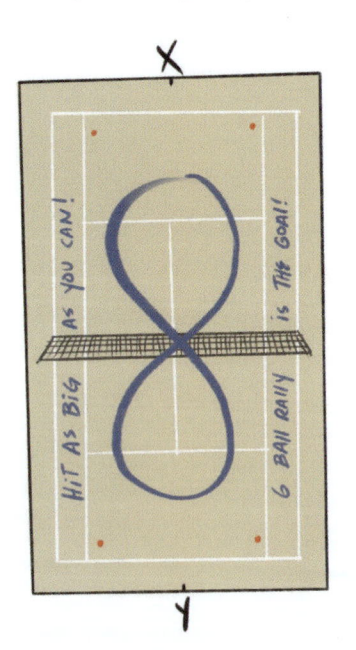

Matches against your equal, or players that are 'better' than you, typically hinge on a couple of points and can be the difference between making or missing a couple of shots you usually wouldn't. For example, how many times have you played a point where somehow you stayed alive in the point and three shots later you won the point; we need to do something special to win points like these. The hard part is that we don't know whether those shots will be a pass, a diving volley, or a great return.

> *One drill I use to practice these types of shots is that I have the players play 'out' balls, and maybe make them worth two points, if you win the point where you play an out ball. This way the players get used to chasing down balls they think are out of their reach; they get good at hitting squash shots and half-volleys from the baseline, and then you see them be able to do it in matches. This drill directly translates into a higher shot tolerance, which is another skill you need when playing your equal or better. Often the momentum of close matches can completely turn after a great volley or out of nowhere pass, converting a couple of these 'hustle' points always helped me feel like I had a chance to win when I was the 'underdog.'*

This book is dedicated to looking for ways to turn 50/50 matchups in our favor. Frequently players try to make their serve and forehand bigger as a way to survive at the 'next level' and overlook and under train the ability to stay alive in points and matches at the higher levels. Many 'average' players who end up constantly cracking through levels have great anticipation and improvisational skills; think about Marco Cecchinato and Jenson Brooksby. They don't have massive weapons, so what allows them to stand out and not only keep improving but keep winning? I believe it's as much their ability to stay alive in points as it is their ability to finish points.

Once you hit the ball well enough to compete at the

ATP level, you can drill taking certain shots into certain zones. **Improvement comes from adding to your skills, not making practices hard for hardness' sake.** Remember that growth and refinement are the main goals, and an intelligent person or player can improve in all but the most brutal scenarios. I try to keep practice scenarios as realistic as possible so that players can obviously see how the drills translate into their game, but as creatively as possible to keep them interested and fight the good fight against monotony and boredom.

Tennis players need to play within a very tight standard deviation from their average level if they want to play tennis in college or on the pro tour. This shows the importance of execution, control, and mastery. There are individual shots that a player just has to be able to hit on a day-to-day basis that need to be practiced. Whether it's countering while on the run with your forehand or taking a backhand down the line; train to get those shots so automatic that you're surprised when you miss one. At the professional level, it seems like we hear about guys having the ability to create offense and execute offense as what gets them into that higher level of competition. So we need to practice that. Rallying endlessly through B&C is excellent, there are tons of things you can work on inside that type of practice, but there are skills you're neglecting if you only build on your B&C game. This is where it's crucial what you and your coach decide to work on and why because both of these practices need to be done. The trick to playing well in tournaments is getting the practice ratio right between developing weapons, playing points, and building skills; that ratio is different for every player.

When I started working with Brandon, we worked on his forehand a lot, his running forehand specifically. It seemed like he would get tangled with his feet and somehow end up too close or too far from the ball, either leaving a short one for his opponent or missing the shot.

So we worked on it in a couple different ways, more or less everyday, and eventually he started to find the rhythm with it and improve.

What we also did, was I'd feed him a backhand, he'd hit it down the line to me, and I'd rip my forehand cross court—getting Brandon on the run to his forehand. He'd then try to create offensive shots with his forehand on the run. Sometimes our goal would be for him to hit '5 into A and D', sometimes I'd let him hit his shot wherever he thought he could, and sometimes we'd just be making the decision of 'offense, defense, or neutral' as he ran to the ball. Getting him able to create offense from the running forehand instantly made his forehand better, and in some cases takes away the need to play defense with it. If he recognizes that he can play offense, then he should do it.

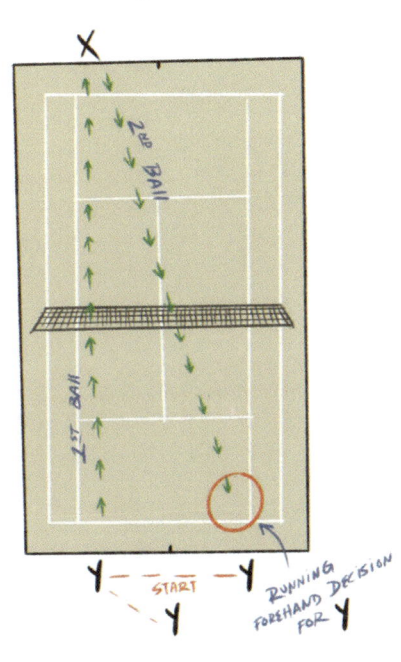

His overall understanding of offense and defense doesn't change depending on his opponent, but his decisions do. We found a shot he needed to improve. We thought about the situation and what his options are in that situation, and then we got to work on it.

SEVEN
MENTALITY OF B+C

Play Like St. Pierre

Tennis is a lot like MMA. A tennis player and an MMA fighter have probably lived very similar lives and have similar outlooks on sports strategy. I don't mean in the obvious ways like that they're both one on one sports, and the burden of outcome is all on the fighter in the ring or player on the court; that being great at either sport might be lonely struggles. Of course, they are similar in those ways, but they're also similar strategically. Georges St. Pierre is a world champion in MMA, many times over, and the last thing on his mind strategically during a fight is to knock his opponent out. I learned a lot about his fighting mentality and how a world-class fighter prepares and thinks when I read his book, "The Way of the Fight."

In his book, St. Pierre broke down his game plan for a world championship fight against Josh Koscheck. St. Pierre wrote, "I start with trying to win a small exchange, maybe two. I want to score some points. After a couple rounds, though, I'm hoping that, like in a chess game, I'm ahead by a few pawns... he'll be forced to take risks... Against Koscheck, I relied on my jab to build my lead, and I expected him to open up...Guys like Mayweather and Hopkins, they'd understood that. Sugar Ray Leonard used his head the same way; he rarely took risks and won a lot of fights."

When I read this part of the book, it became clear to me that St. Pierre was playing the MMA version of B&C. He was so confident in his ability to stay neutral, or slightly offensive that he didn't need to rush offense. He didn't need to go for a knockout. St. Pierre won 26 fights in his Hall of Fame career; 8 by knockout, six by submission, and 12 by decision. He could knock people out, but that wasn't his strategy or his 'option A.' I would say more tennis matches at the pro level are 'won by decision' rather than by 'knockout.'

In tennis, if you're not prepared to win the match through B&C you will need things to go your way either all match or in a couple of critical moments for you to win. That's not a reality you want to face too often. While training B&C, it's vital to understand that you're working on your mentality and decision making as much as you're working on your strokes. You are throwing jabs, constantly looking for weaknesses and opportunities to attack, but you're throwing jabs first and foremost. Your intent is to be offensive, but in the most controlled, confident way possible. **If you walk on court feeling like you can beat your opponent playing a high percentage strategy, without needing a miracle, you'll be truly confident.** Now you're in control. You feel like the opponent will need things to go their way to beat you in the match. That's the kind of pressure you want your opponent to feel and the kind of confidence you want to feel.

Once a player believes that 'throwing jabs' will help her win matches and have the type of career she wants, her training changes. She's now playing points almost all day, looking for balls to attack on. The player will begin anticipating what her opponent will most likely do while staying inside B&C. That will put her in more offensive situations without adding any risk to her everyday style of play.

Let's say you're hitting a backhand a couple feet behind the baseline, in your D, but everything's fine, it's a rally ball—you play it cross, and he takes a BH line into your B, now you're moving to your forehand, and you'll get to it, but you're on the run. Now, what's your best option? Your best option is to play your forehand line into his C and then anticipate he goes BH cross into your C, and then if that ball sits up, you can try and play offense with your BH. This type of thinking is what you can do when you understand percentages and where shots go—as well as agree that staying inside B&C is roughly 90% of the time going to be your best option.

Having a coach who can understand your strengths and weaknesses and how to best use them, is key. This type of coach can stand behind the player and help them see the patterns and opportunities for offense that the player may not be aware of. **Getting to this stage with a player is key because now almost all practice time is instantly applicable to match situations. Now the player sees the practice as fine-tuning for matches. This is where full engagement happens. The dialogue between player and coach about what shots were available and which weren't is when the player starts to truly take in the information and feel the game.**

The best players feel the game better than others. Having 'feel' for the game, is slang for 'mental representation.' Players 'feel' the game, similarly to St.Pierre saying, 'I want to score some points. After a couple rounds, though, I'm hoping that, like in a chess game, I'm ahead by a few pawns... he'll be forced to take risks.' The players with the best 'feel', or mental representation, for the game, know what's likely to happen, what's not and then how to deal with both; they're almost always one step ahead of their opponents. They try to get 'ahead by a few pawns' before they go for the King. This is how being smarter against your equal can earn you offensive opportunities without necessarily having a bigger serve or forehand.

B&C Collaboration

For the college or pro player, B&C should be done at game speed and game mentality. This way, the player can hear feedback from the coach that is 100% applicable to a match. The player will now know what the coach is thinking during matches, and what adjustments he may think the player should make, which helps for matches when the player and coach can't talk. It's crucial that the player and coach are in the same mentality during this scenario so that they're on the same page about what is trying to be accomplished. If the player thinks it's 'just practice' and the coach thinks it's 'competition,' then their communication will break down and probably make the practice less productive.

The best practices happen when players and coaches are in the same mentality-communication is smooth and almost doesn't need to be said. This is the ideal space for learning, growth, and enjoyment. This is flow.

So often in tennis, we communicate about injuries, string tension, how the court is playing, etc. but we rarely talk about our mentality. The mental side of tennis is no longer of unknown value; it's a significant part of winning tennis matches, and we need to consciously work on it as we do other parts of our physical game. To me, this is why coach-player relationships are better off as collaborations; we both have to communicate about our intensity level that day. We have to talk about what we want to accomplish and be honest with each other, accept each other, and work to find a middle ground if we are not on the same page at a given practice session. Giving our best effort to improve has to be the baseline. Any player or coach who is dogging it won't make it anyway, but shouldn't waste the other person's time.

Getting into a competitive mindset while drilling is massive because what else is there to do when looking to break through to a new level? You've got to always be looking for balls to hit bigger, for balls to move forward and take away time, for adjustments that could be made, if you want to be an offensive player. At this point in your career, your opponents aren't missing when on the run; it's not like going 2 cross 1 line works anymore. Everyone's fit, everyone is more or less your equal. **When you're drilling B&C, you're learning to manage a point and how to best play neutral balls—the handling of which truly separates the players of different levels.** Players that engage in the mental side of B&C are getting good at managing shot selection and the most common balls they'll see during matches; those who choose not to engage are simply hitting through the middle. **The level of mental-engagement by the player determines the value of the drill.**

A variation on B&C that I like to do is to open up the court and allow for balls to land anywhere, but the last ball must be played through C. Players can use angles, or go for winners, whatever they want to do, but they don't earn a point unless the last ball played lands in C. C is the area of the court where most points end; making it the most valuable spot on the court. It may take a while to earn a point, so play to 5. This game, with this rule, teaches players how to play the minimums, and it directs their focus to the most valuable spot on the court, which makes them smarter players whether they know it or not. It teaches players to go to A&D with control, because they WANT their opponent to get to it so they can play the next ball through C. Players will end up exchanging heavy, deep, flat, low, high, slice shots, and pushing the limits of what they can do with the ball, all while playing the most aggressive, 'pro-style' game they can. There are many levels to this drill, many more than an unaware onlooker would notice, so it's even more important that the player and coach are in the same mentality while doing it.

I don't know if practicing with this mentality will work for everyone, but I know that practicing mindlessly works for no one. I set up practices for my players with a focus on practicing skills-not correcting missed shots. Being skilled and tactical allows the player to have consistent results and gives them an opportunity to have the types of careers they want.

While practicing like this, players are learning to read the flight of the ball, to register its speed, spin, and depth. Better players hit the ball faster, heavier, deeper, and with more control and generally higher racket head speed because they have fired those neural pathways more efficiently than the players at lower levels. **Players are building myelin always, whether it's with their thoughts or actions, so if they practice how to think, they'll get better at thinking. Controlling one's thoughts is every bit as important as maintaining one's body. It's all hand-in-hand.**

EIGHT
TALKIN BOUT PRACTICE

Many of us tennis players practice the same shots, do the same drills, with the same thoughts in mind, year after year, basically hoping something will 'click.' This may work for some people, but how many people really improve in their careers? I'd say most people get better simply because they get older, stronger, and more mature on court. To me, this shouldn't be the case. **Practice is for learning new skills and growing your game mentally, physically, and emotionally.**

When warming up, players should be thinking about hitting the ball as cleanly as they can. They're getting their eyes used to tracking the flight of the ball, and their bodies used to moving again. You're working with your practice partner in this warmup situation, so make sure you're hitting a ball that they can easily hit back to you. You're not trying to win the warmup rallies. Pick a depth in the court and a height over the net you want to hit, and get it every time. This way, you're warming up your eyes, brain, and body while learning how to hit the ball as clean as possible. You'll get in-sync with the ball in the most critical ways.

After warming up, you can start doing drills. To me, there are two types of exercises— movement drills and decision making drills. Movement drills are patterned drills, like 2 cross 1 line, or one player dictating out of one corner and the other player covering their whole side. Movement drills like this allow the player and coach to think about footwork, or spacing, or make some technical adjustment to their swing. They're quite literally going through the motions, growing habits, and myelin. Decision-making drills are for putting players in realistic match situations and working on their decisions; train them to think strategically and understand risk.

Man on the Run

Movement drills are great for working on being on the run or getting in and out of the corners efficiently. It's all about either fine-tuning your swings or footwork into the ball, or it's basically conditioning and fitness training on court in a hitting situation. Always work on moving up and back in the court as well as side to side; great players can cover the entire court.

I like movement scenarios because it can give the players freedom to work on a ton of different skills with the right mindset. Let's say one player is dictating out of his forehand corner, moving the other player around. The player who's dictating can work on playing shots at the limit of the other player's reach—pushing him just enough to struggle, but not so much that he can only scrape balls back into the court. This is a great way to learn the value of playing the minimums while on offense.

As the dictator in this drill, you can see how difficult it is for your partner to be on defense, and that it would take a miraculous shot for him to turn the tables. You're in control of the rally, you need to maintain that amount of control, and sooner or later, you'll either have a wide-open court to hit into, or your partner will miss. You don't need to force the error. Once the dictating player feels the control and can understand how to use it, they can begin to play like that in matches. It's all about understanding the scenario and what the best strategy is. Slowing it down, or isolating it, as we do in this scenario by having one player dictate from the forehand side, is a great way to show the players these intricacies. As the legendary football coach, Tom Martinez, says, "It's not how fast you can do it. It's how slow you can do it correctly." I love applying this quote to tennis because to beat your equal consistently, you've got to have your skills mastered, and this type of practice is how athletes in all different sports become masters.

There is always something to work on, and especially when you're drilling with another player, you've got to have value in both positions. You don't want to set up scenarios where only one player is benefitting, and the other is simply the 'hitter' too often. So, the player being dictated to in this drill could think, 'Ok, this is like being in a match where nothing is going right. I'm going to try and use the weight of my ball to keep me alive, and I'm going to play through his weaker side.' That's a great mentality to practice in because it happens all the time in real matches. So now you're practicing your gameplan for when things aren't going your way. You're going to hit every ball as cleanly as you can, as heavy as you can, to his weaker side. That is absolutely a gameplan worth working on.

You can also work on countering in this drill, as the player being dictated to. The moving player may have a mindset like, 'Ok, this guy is bullying me around the court, and I can't go side to side like this all day. I've got to try and counter if I get an opportunity.' Now, the player moves side to side while looking for a ball to inject pace on and try to earn a short ball from the dictator. This is how you develop turning defense into offense in one shot. It's all about recognizing the right ball to try nd do it on, and then having the skill to do it. There are nearly endless variations of skills you can work on inside of this drilling set up that are valuable for both players. **It depends what you're focused on and how much of your imagination you're willing to use.**

Decisions Decisions

The decisions you make on court determine the outcome of the match against your equal; every shot presents a new set of decisions for us to make and hopefully get correct. All the drills in this section are based around decision-making and ball recognition in alignment with the percentages of how pros use ABCD and their understanding of playing the minimums. Ball recognition means that you see what shots are available on any given ball and you choose the best one given your strengths, weaknesses, and the score at the time. Every player is different and needs to decide for themselves what are good and bad decisions given their playing style; this is where having a coach you trust and are on the same page with becomes crucial. **Consistently making better decisions will help you win matches and compete at a higher level with less fluctuation in your game.**

For example, a drill I love is to have players play singles points where you lose the point if you hit three backhands in a row. This gets players looking to hit their forehand and targeting their opponent's backhand. So now the player and coach are looking at the flight of the ball, and seeing if the player is missing balls that sit up for a split second and could be hit more aggressively; maybe you missed a chance to inject pace, or perhaps you could've played a forehand instead of a backhand. Maybe you played a ball down the line when you could've gotten more out of going cross-court. This is where it's all about looking for strategic use of your shots, risk-management and execution.

Drill: Play regular singles points, looking for opportunities to use your backhand down the line.
Player: Your goal in this drill is to play points as 'normally' as possible. You want to be close to game speed here in terms of how you're hitting the ball, your movement, and your decision making. Your emphasis is to try and either earn more backhands where going down the line is the right play by moving your opponent around, or you want to work on pulling the trigger and trying to catch your opponent off guard when you go line. Be clear with what you're trying to do.
Coach: Your goal in this drill is to be the player's second set of eyes. You are looking at the flight of the ball, seeing if your player could have taken any ball down the line. You want to watch the opponent and see how he reacts to certain shots from your player; maybe there is a pattern your player could use that he doesn't see. Potentially the opponent doesn't like when your player slices to his backhand. He sometimes leaves that ball sitting up, and that's the one your player should take line. Slice and sting, baby. You can then tell the player about the pattern and help him be more aware of the opportunities going on on the court.

Another realistic ball recognition drill I love is to have one player hitting inside out forehands through C, and the other player hitting slice backhands back through C at different depths and speeds. The forehand player is looking for the right ball to pull inside-in through a window set up in A&B, trying to get to five. This will teach the forehand player how to get into the right position to hit that shot, which type of a slice to take that shot off of and which to play back through C, and they'll also work on one of the more difficult shots in the game all at the same time.

How to Tennis

(INSIDE OUT FOREHANDS) X

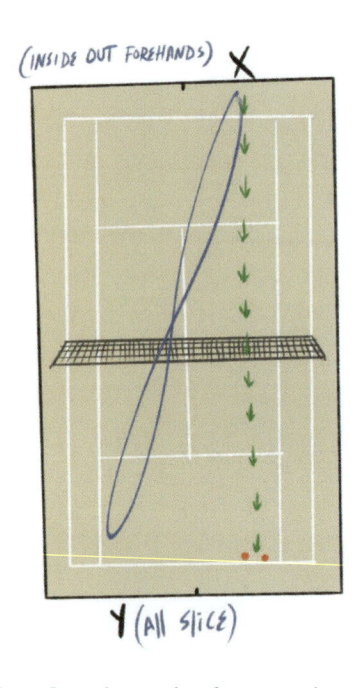

Y (All slice)

    This gives the forehand player time to think about how he likes his body to be, and if he likes taking slices off his shoelaces through the window or if he's better off waiting for one that's more around knee height. He can use that information to help him with his decision-making in matches. When his opponent hits a slice into C, and he's in a forehand inside out position, he'll either go inside in or inside out based on what he trained in practice and what he recognizes in his opponent's slice. **It's allowing your ball recognition to be your guiding factor in what shots you decide to play that is the key**. You minimize your risk by grouping balls together in this way and simultaneously clear your mind of running through the four different options of shots to hit that you are used to seeing.

Threshold Pushers

    Every practice should have some threshold to push as a goal. In his best-selling book, "The Talent Code,"

Daniel Coyle writes, 'The trick is to choose a goal just beyond your present abilities; to target the struggle. Thrashing blindly doesn't help. Reaching does.' Coyle calls this 'the sweet spot of learning,' and suggests later on in the book that we should continuously challenge ourselves by 4% to maximize our learning and growth potential. This idea works on several different levels and in different practices, but I suggest reading his book for the more scientific breakdown of how this training method leads to improvement. I use his ideas as guides and have read the books I quote from multiple times, as I go on my own path of trying to help each player I work with succeed and go toward their potentials.

Pushing the limits of what you do and growing skills should be fun. Getting back to tennis, let's say you want to push the limits of your fitness, you can do a ton of dictating and 1 cross 1 line; or maybe you want to work on serve technique, so you have to do the same movement over and over again, pushing your ability to focus on one small movement. Maybe you're practicing something you're bad at, for the sole intention of pushing your threshold of when you start to get tired—you can teach yourself not to get frustrated, or overly excited, or whatever you want, if you consciously think about working on it.

Pushing our mental threshold is important because our minds win and lose us many matches. We go to the gym to get stronger because we know it's possible to get stronger and we know it will help us be better at tennis. We can do the same thing for our brains. We just have to think of the 'mental workouts' we need.

Let's say you have a habit of letting off the gas when you're winning, and you turn 'easy wins' into tight nail biters, or even worse, losses. You want to get better at closing out matches. So, you could practice playing sets from up 4-1. You are practicing being focused while you have a lead and not letting down. You're reinforcing to yourself that you can and do focus when you're up in the score. It's more than visualization; it's all about the myelin. You put yourself in the situation you typically fail in, and then you figure out how to succeed in it.

As Coyle writes, 'struggling in certain targeted ways—operating at the edges of your ability, where you make mistakes—makes you smarter.' You're struggling closing out matches, so practice that. Fifteen more minutes of forehands cross court won't help you hold your nerve any better in tight moments. No amount of physical work can make up for the mental work that needs to be done, and vice versa. **Mental parts of tennis can be worked on, it just requires a bit of imagination on the player's part.**

Communicate Clearly

Another thing about practice that's massive, especially when working with a new coach or player, is being on the same page with your words. There are a million ways to interpret sayings like, 'You gotta rip that one,' or 'You gotta manage that ball better.' So we've got to be clear about the meaning of the words we use; many practices are ruined because of miscommunication between player and coach. Here are some keywords I use during practices, and my definition for them—feel free to take em or leave em.

Variance: Variance is accuracy. Let's say I put up a cone on the cross-court forehand side, then how accurate a player is over X number of shots aiming at that cone, is that player's variance with their cross-court forehand. You can figure out and test variance with every shot. Figuring out a player's variance is important because then the coach knows what standard to hold them to, and the player understands how much margin they need to give themselves while playing. How can you go for a shot that has to be inch-perfect in the most crucial moment of a match, if your variance is 5 feet? Understanding your own variance, and being disciplined enough to play within it, will instantly cut down on your errors and make you a more difficult opponent to beat.

I also run practices and form my expectations based on the player's variance. Misses, to me, are only those balls that fall outside the player's variance. Let's say you have a 5-foot variance on your inside in forehand—and now you get the right ball to take inside in, you give it the right speed, spin, shape, you get the depth correct, but you miss the shot one foot wide. To me, that's not a miss. That's just a reminder of your variance. After a player misses that shot, I might say something like, 'Ok, you set it up right. It was the right ball. We've just got to keep working on getting the variance tighter and tighter on this shot.' Basing makes and misses around the individual player's variance makes theories easier to understand and keeps the player and coach honest about what they're really doing and what can be expected.

Intent: I assume pro players are in control of every shot they hit: I think they mean to put an exact amount of speed, spin, height, depth on every shot. If I'm going to study them and give this and that player credit for doing this and that on court, then I have to assume he's consciously doing what he's doing. Intent is exactly what it sounds like; it's the player's intent with X shot. 'Did you mean to hit it there?' 'Were you going for a two-pass combo or an outright winner pass?' It's essential to be on the same page about a shot's intention because that's how the player and coach know what adjustments to make. If you went for a winner and missed, but could've won the point by just making that shot a bit safer, then it's the player's decision to go for the winner there that needs to be talked about, not necessarily the technical thing that happened that made your shot miss wide. Let's say you meant to just roll in a kick serve, but instead, you hit a slice, and it went long, then it's more of a technical adjustment you need to look into. Understanding intent can save you hours of frustration on court and allow you to make corrections as quickly as possible, making you better and your practice time more efficient. It takes honesty and a willingness to be vulnerable, go for it.

Ball Recognition: You rarely see the same ball twice, so getting good at ball recognition is key to being a great player. To me, ball recognition is knowing what shots are available to you with each ball your opponent plays. The best players in the world recognize the ball coming towards them, and the options it has for them, quicker than the rest of us. You can almost always be working on your ball recognition, no matter the drill. Can you inject pace? Can you change directions? Can you go to A? All these thoughts need to go through your mind on every shot, but it's got to get to a point where you don't have to have those thoughts consciously—but they become second nature and happen without you trying. That's where you want to get with your ball recognition skills.

Mentality: I believe that you can make up ground on those players just ahead of you if you change your mentality. How often do we look at physical parts of our game, hoping to gain ground on our opponents, and how often do we look at mental aspects of our game to gain an advantage? To me, there is an almost entirely untapped reserve in most of our mental games that could take us to a new level. If you haven't rethought your approach to your career, I'd recommend starting there before messing with your forehand technique.

Rip: This is a common word thrown around tennis courts all over the world, but what does it mean? Player and coach need to be on the same page with what they mean when they say common words like this—to me, ripping means hitting your controlled rally ball bigger than you normally would. To actually rip, you've got to be in control; so it's a very subtle difference between your normal swing and when you're 'ripping' It doesn't necessarily mean you're hitting more winners or hitting the ball much faster than you usually do, it's subtle and control-based.

Manage: Most shots in tennis are 'managed.' This is another way of saying most of the time, you're neutral. You are in control of the shot, and have options of how to hit it, but the first thing in your mind is making the shot. 'Managing the shot' means you did what you could do with it while keeping making it and continuing the point your main goal. A half-volley is a shot that needs to be managed. You can make it, and sometimes you can hit a great shot with a half-volley, but for the most part, you've got to manage it and take care of it.**Competitive**: There is such a thing as 'being a good competitor.' At every level of the game, there are people who do not have the strokes or the shot-making ability to play at their level, but somehow they win matches. They figure out how to win with what they've got. That is a skill that can be learned. Once you know what you're good at, and you get very good at it, then you can figure out how you could win with what you've got. Being a good competitor is crucial to reaching your potential because you can win many matches with your 'C Game' if your head game is an A. A classic example of a great competitor is David Ferrer. Watch his matches, and you'll see that his greatest weapons are his competitive spirit and brain, not his shots.

A good competitor to me is a person who is willing to consider almost anything to get better, and ready to look at his own game from an outside perspective to improve as a player overall. Whether that's a new coach, a new diet, a new technique, doesn't matter. Everything has room for improvement and should be looked into.

You also need to be competitive with the other players. I think there is some part of the best sportsmen that does flat out want to be the best. They want to literally be the greatest ever. But that desire should also be measured and harnessed. Being too cocky is just as bad as being too doubtful of yourself. Whether you're cocky or insecure, both ways of thinking have flaws in them. That's why you've got to be competitive with yourself, always trying to check for deficiencies in your perception. This way keeps you as confident as possible because it keeps you honest, and you'll be most confident when you are honest.

Practice: Time to learn and grow. The coach should have practices prepared for the player to go through. Players should add their thoughts, recommend ways of making it better or adding/subtracting certain things. Practice time should be a collaboration between player and coach; both have different views on what the player needs, so both should have a say in what happens on the practice court. It shouldn't be the place for convincing the player to try hard or engage in the practice. That is a given. That is the player's responsibility, just as the coach has to engage and try hard. It's all the same. Every role has it's good and bad parts, and all have to be played all the time.

Mental Representation: Your mental representation is what you see when you look at or imagine a situation on court. Better players have a better mental representation of the situation they're in on court. They therefore are more likely to figure out the solution to it than less skilled and experienced players. Adjusting your mental representation can be one of the most significant areas of improvement for an already skilled player.

Tennis IQ: To me, is how a player sees the game. Tennis players with a high Tennis IQ are almost always considering the scoring situation of the moment, what their opponent's tendencies and capabilities are and how they match up against their own game. They seem to have a super power of always making the right decisions through various different situations on court.

NINE
CONCLUSION

In my experiences with tennis so far, I've seen a lot. I've been part of the game at almost every level, from teaching three-year-olds to playing Futures in Azerbaijan and most recently working with players inside the Top 100 of the world rankings, and what sticks out to me the most is that what you're good at is what you should do. **You should embrace and grow the skills that make you unique on a tennis court.** Mastery of individual skills will help you establish a game plan that you can rely on and use to beat your equals as well as reach your potential.

I haven't seen that many players change; for fun, watch some clips on YouTube of Nadal, Cilic and DelPotro from their junior days in the 'Under 14' divisions - they have almost identical games to how they play now, except now they're grown men. Those guys have ball-striking ability that not many people on the planet have, but it is interesting to see how similar they are now to when they were juniors. There is certainly something to the idea of working with what you've got, and not always trying to rework your game - grow your skillset and your tennis IQ before you reconsider all your techniques.

I've worked with and seen players obsess over techniques and grips only to end up a month down the road with little to show for their work hours. I've also seen players with funky techniques and gnarly grips become some of the world's best players and do more with tennis than anyone expected. **There are many ways to reach your potential in tennis, but there are no cheat codes**.

The players who improve the most and get close to their potential are the players who work for it. To be clear, just working out hard and having tough practice sessions is not what I mean when I say that the players 'work for it.' Improvement comes from looking into all aspects of your game that you will need at the level you want to get to and then coming up with ways to master those different areas. **I think many tennis players would reach their potential quicker if they traded in an hour per week of physical practice for an hour of thought.** Think about how the game is played at the level you want to get to, the strategies involved, the skills required. Think about what you're trying to do, and come up with ways to improve those areas.

The ideas I've laid out in this book are nothing more than a guide and a look into how I view tennis. I may not be right, and I'm certainly not going to be the right coach for every player—but that's ok. Everyone learns and thinks differently and should be treated as such. This book captures how I think and some of the ways I believe tennis players can train, but it will be continually evolving for as long as I stay in tennis. There is no black and white guide to reaching your potential; it will take trial and error to find what works for you.

Many of the ideas I've put down here have come from moments when I felt 'burned out' as a player, or watched as other players go through the motions their coaches put them through with no passion or interest. Too much drilling. Too many patterns. Never-ending hoppers of balls. A large part of winning tennis matches is problem-solving, and each player will find different solutions to similar problems. To me, this shows the player's creativity, their understanding of strategy, and how they use their strengths and weaknesses on the court; I hate to see a player get their creativity 'drilled' out of them. Players should enjoy being on the court; they have to want to be out there week after week, tournament after tournament; enjoying life off-court is a big part of success on it.

As I've written this book, I've been nearly obsessive about tennis over the last three years, not just thinking about how my playing career went, but how other players I've known have done. I've thought about all the coaches I've seen, all the hours on court I've been a part of, and I've tried to piece together the ideal environment for a player to improve. What is the best way to get across to players, and what's the best way for players to get their points across to coaches? Is there a strategy that works for everyone? How great it would be if I had found that magic, but I haven't yet.

The most common trait the best players and coaches I've noticed have is that they are fully engaged with their careers. They work hard, for sure. They enjoy what they're doing, for sure. They have good and bad days, for sure. But no matter what day you catch them on, they are engaged with their career. Borderline obsessive, but more so enthusiastic and interested. This comes across in different ways, some coaches seem 'smart' while others seem more 'laid-back' and some players seem 'scrappy' and others seem 'nonchalant'; the styles are different, everyone has their quirks, but as I've looked through my journals of notes about this game, I've been reminded about how this and that player and coaches' level of engagement stood out to me. It's not merely energy that these people have, nor is it some amount of tennis IQ that most of us can't reach - it's a genuine interest in improvement and honest engagement with the practice at hand.

This level of engagement I'm talking about is what makes going after your potential so fun, because no matter what your style of playing or coaching is, you can probably find a way to reach your potential. That's why there are coaches who yell and berate their players at the top of the game as well as coaches that believe in Zen Buddhism and yet others who believe tennis is 'just a game to have fun with.' We've all got to find the mentality and physical surroundings that foster our growth in a style that feels authentic to us and then fully engage with our careers.

Think of how to best play and practice your game, do that, and leave the rest aside. There are not any secrets better players than you know that you don't. This game can be won in many different ways; tennis is not black and white. Use the information in this book to shape the way you practice and compete, and see if it helps guide you towards your potential, for me that's the most rewarding thing we all get from this great sport, the opportunity to go after our potential.

BIBLIOGRAPHY

I've read more books and articles than I can remember about tennis and sport and mastery, and all of them have helped shape my thoughts. Here are some of my recommendations and a look into what's in my tennis bag while on the road or on my shelves at home.

Coyle, Daniel. *The Talent Code: Unlocking the Secret of Skill in Sports, Art, Music, Math, and Just about Anything.* Bantam Books, 2009.

Gallwey, W. Timothy. *The Inner Game of Tennis.* Random House, 2008.

Gilbert, Brad, and Steve Jamison. *Winning Ugly: Mental Warfare in Tennis--Lessons from a Master.* Simon & Schuster, 2013.

Gladwell, Malcolm. *What the Dog Saw.* Back Bay Books, 2009.

Kotler, Steven. *The Rise of Superman: Decoding the Science of Ultimate Human Performance.* New Harvest, 2014.

Syed, Matthew. *The Greatest: What Sport Teaches Us About Achieving Success.* John Murray Press, 2017.

Sinek, Simon. *The Infinite Game.* Penguin, 2019.

Printed in Great Britain
by Amazon